With Mo
from HPB

Front cover
View of the Abbot's house, c. 1748, by Thomas
Robins the elder. National Trust.

View of the ruins of Hailes Abbey from the air.

ENGLISH HERITAGE

HAILES: THE STORY OF A GLOUCESTERSHIRE ABBEY

by
Doreen Winkless

The Spredden Press

First published 1990 by
The Spredden Press
Stocksfield
Northumberland

Reissued by
English Heritage 2001

ISBN 1 871739 14 4

First printed and bound by
SMITH SETTLE
Ilkley Road, Otley, West Yorkshire LS21 3JP

This edition printed by
PRINTCO
6/7 West Avenue, Walthamstow, London E17 9QN

CONTENTS

Acknowledgements

List of Illustrations

1.   The Founder of Hailes Abbey

2.   The Foundation and Building of the Monastery

3.   The Holy Blood

4.   The Early Years of the Monastery

5.   Hailes Parish Church

6.   The Middle Years

7.   Recovery

8.   The Last Days of Hailes

References

Select Bibliography

ACKNOWLEDGEMENTS

I should like to thank all those who over many years have taken so much time and trouble to help me trace and collect much of the material of this book. In particular, I am very grateful to Nancy Pringle for her work in the Local Collections of Cheltenham Reference Library and the facilities placed at our disposal there, also to Gloucester City Library where the many boxes of the Baddeley Collection were brought out again and again for our examination. In this and the work of deciphering and translating the chronicles of Hailes Abbey I owe a great debt to the following who worked with me so cheerfully and enthusiastically: Nita Arnott, Peggy Booth, Margaret Currall, Janet Chanin, Joan Dell, Margaret Ellison, Margaret Fisher, Margaret Keith, Keith Keeley, Stanley Jarman, Jean Judd, Audrey, Medlicott, Winifred Mills, Joy Mules, Nancy Payne, Beryl Pullan. Margery Smith, Ruth Troughton, Carole Clifford and the late Jean Hearn, Coleen Martin, Peter Booth and Dr Jean Jenkins.

I should also like to acknowledge the help given by the late John Horlick of Didbrook for making available his transcript of the Hailes Parish Register and the notebook of St Aubyn Weston (1897); Charles Hoby for his kindness in making available family papers; Meredith Sassoon for keeping me in touch with her research on the encaustic tiles of Hailes; Sue and Neil Greenhalf who have never failed to welcome me and my enquiries at Hailes; the Hon. Mrs Guy Charteris for her enthusiastic support and for letting me read her late husband's papers, and Lord Sudeley who for a decade has unfailingly channelled to me any information which might throw light on the history of the abbey and especially on its association with the Tracy family. To all these I owe very grateful thanks indeed.

A very special thank you is due to Bruce Francis and his wife Evelyn, for their enthusiastic interest and encouragement and for much practical help. Bruce Francis not only took many of the photographs in the book but also typed and ordered the text which his wife carefully checked with him. I have been very fortunate that their love of Hailes has brought such benefit to me.

I would also like to thank the following for permission to publish photographs of objects in their possession: The National Trust for the watercolour by Thomas Robins (cover); The Dean and Chapter of Wells, for the page from the Hailes Psalter, now in Wells Cathedral; The Gloucester Record Office for the Seal of Hailes Abbey; The British Museum for the Seal of the Confraternity of Hailes; The Public Record Office for the Tally sticks; and Skyscan for the view of Hailes from the air (frontispiece).

Lastly I remember with great affection and gratitude my late husband who spent countless hours sitting in the cloisters at Hailes, waiting and thinking in great happiness and serenity.

Leckhampton, 1990

ILLUSTRATIONS

	Page
View of the ruins of Hailes Abbey from the air.	Frontispiece
13th-century boss showing Christ as a spiritual Samson rending the lion's jaw.	10
13th-century vaulting bosses found in the Chapter House, now in the Abbey Museum.	13
15th-century bosses found in the Chapter House.	14
Ground plan of the chevet from the north-east, showing the base of the shrine and its encircling pillars. Cloister arches visible in the background.	18
Seal of the Confraternity of Hailes.	26
The west range of the cloister when it was the home of the Tracy family. View by Kip, c1712.	29
Tally sticks. The second from the top came from Pinnock.	30
St Catherine. 14th-century in the splay of the north chancel window.	35
14th-century paintings of strange creatures in the spandrels of the chancel windows in the church.	37
Tiles from east end of church, c. 1270.	37
Scal of Hailes Abbey 1425.	40
Psalm 1 in the Hailes Psalter, written by Peter Meghen in 1514, now in Wells Cathedral Library. The arms are those of Christopher Urswyck. Dean and Chapter of Wells.	52

The cloister from the east.   65

Victorian visitors from a London archaeological society seen   66
near the west cloister walk. *Illustrated Times,* 16 August
1856.

1. THE FOUNDER OF HAILES ABBEY

I have not my peer in England, for I am the son of the late king and brother of the present one and I am also Earl of Cornwall. *Matthew Paris*, 13th century

He was a prince both expert and valiant in war and so solid in Council that what fortune denied him in battle he supplied in his conduct and advice. *Holinshed*, 16th century

His style was 'Richard, King of the Romans and Alemayne, Earl of Poitiers and Cornwall' *Sandford*, 18th century

In 1242 a storm-tossed ship, separated from the rest of the fleet, found safety on the coast of the Scilly Isles off Cornwall. On board was Richard, Earl of Cornwall, son of King John and brother of King Henry III. According to tradition, Richard in his time of danger had vowed to build a new abbey if God would save him from the perils of the storm. He kept that vow and so the Cistercian abbey of Hailes in Gloucestershire was built.

The story of Hailes must begin with some account of its founder and his family for without his wealth and patronage and that of his second son, Edmund, there would be no story to tell. Richard's arms appear in 13th- and 16th-century encaustic tiles found at Hailes, living proof that the monks never forget their founder in the near three centuries of their existence. In the little parish church just beyond the abbey boundaries his arms and those of his three wives and a number of their relations can still be seen painted on the walls, while high up in the east window there survives, in ancient glass, a somewhat defaced shield of the arms of the Earldom of Cornwall.

Born in 1209, Richard was the second son of King John and Isabella of Angoulême, a stormy heritage. His elder brother became Henry III. Richard was named after his warrior uncle, Coeur de Lion, a name that gained him prestige in his own crusading days. Richard secured the release of French prisoners from an earlier unsuccessful expedition to the Holy Land, thereby gaining the enduring respect of the French,[1] but his main achievement was to be in the field of diplomacy. He arranged a truce which gained access for pilgrims to Jerusalem and the Holy Places and left behind at

Ascalon elaborate fortifications which were to serve as a defensive base for further crusades. Richard's early years had been spent at Corfe Castle in Dorset and this may have inspired his life-long interest in castle building. His work survives at Tintagel and Launceston while records of Wallingford Castle indicate his family's activities there.

Richard married three times and these marriages provided important spheres of influence in the realm and outside. His first wife was Isabella Marshall (widow of his friend Gilbert de Clare, Earl of Gloucester) by whom he had a son, Henry, whose tragic death was to hasten his own. His second marriage was to Sanchia of Provence whose sisters married the Kings of England, France and Sicily; by this marriage Richard had a son, Edmund, who gave Hailes its famous and much venerated relic of the Holy Blood. Lastly he married Beatrix von Falkenburg (or Valkenburg), niece of the Archbishop of Cologne. All three wives were reputed to be women of outstanding beauty. Isabella died in childbirth, Sanchia after a lingering illness and Beatrix briefly outlived her husband.

King Henry heaped honours on his younger brother adding the title of Count of Poitou to that of Cornwall: the French king later reclaimed the title.[2] Another and more prestigious title came later when Richard was elected King of the Romans, an intermediate step towards election as Holy Roman Emperor.[3]

Richard's influence through family connections was enormous.[4] He was also a very rich man, with vast revenues from his many estates but particularly from those in Cornwall and the tin mines. Other lucrative appointments came his way, especially the responsibility for the reform of the coinage and weights and measures. This involved calling in all the old clipped, debased, short-cross coins and minting new ones where the cross extended over the border to inhibit fraudulent clipping.[5] It was a tedious process; unfortunate citizens had to find their way to a limited number of centres for re-coining and then wait their turn, paying thirteen pence for every pound weight of the work done. They naturally viewed the whole operation with jaundiced eyes! Matthew Paris, who became very indignant about anything to do with taxation, wrote:

> They were reduced to great straits and suffered no slight injury in as much as twenty shillings was scarcely obtained from money changers for thirty not counting the trouble and expense of several days duration and tedious expectation.

Such goings-on did nothing for Richard's popularity in England but they certainly helped fill his treasury. The whole operation of the new coinage and weights and measures is estimated to have brought in some twenty thousand pounds. This windfall came just as Richard was building his new abbey at Hailes. Yet another source of revenue was added when the Pope granted the Earl the right to collect crusading dues.

Richard's vow to build an abbey may well have been made after the shipwreck of 1242 and in 1245 his brother, the King, gave him the manor of Hailes in Gloucestershire expressly for the purpose of building a new monastery. Work seems to have begun almost at once. In the next chapter it will be shown that the scale and manner of the building were to fit the Earl's wealth and influence. By 1251 it was ready for solemn dedication. Richard and most of his family were to have the privilege of burial there and indeed lie there still.

The period following the building of Hailes, however, was to be a troubled one for the country and for Richard. His diplomatic skill was frequently called upon during the many disputes between the King and his subjects. The Earl was by no means always an uncritical supporter of his brother's actions, especially during the period of his first marriage with its baronial connections, but he remained fundamentally loyal to the royal cause when open warfare broke out, and he was present at the disastrous Battle of Lewes (1264) when he, his son Edmund and the King were all taken prisoner. They were sent to Kenilworth Castle under the charge of their victor, Simon de Montfort's wife — another of their married sisters.[6] For this reason Richard was not present at the Battle of Evesham the following year which led to the defeat, death and mutilation of Simon de Montfort.

De Montfort's death cast a long shadow over Richard of Cornwall's life, for it led to the murder of his heir, Henry, by the sons of de Montfort.[7] The murder at Viterbo in Italy took place in circumstances similar to those of Thomas Becket a century earlier. It made a vivid impact on contemporaries and was seen as revenge for Simon's death, although neither Richard nor Henry had been at Evesham. The monk who wrote the Hailes chronicle described the murderers as 'two satellites of Satan' who hacked down Henry as he knelt at prayer before the altar of the church at Viterbo. Other sources describe the 'two enemies of the human race' entering the church with drawn swords, pounding down the nave with clash of armour and reaching their victim as two deacons tried to raise him to his feet. A mighty sword-thrust split Henry's skull while a second blow hacked at the hand clinging to the altar so that some of his fingers and flesh adhered to it. Dante in his *Divine Comedy*, written within a decade of this horrific event, places the spirit of the young Guy de Montfort in the seventh circle of Hell. Henry's intestines were buried in Italy 'between two Popes' but his heart was carried to England for burial in Westminster Abbey near the shrine of Edward the Confessor: in Dante's words, 'the heart which yet is honoured on the bank of Thames'. His bones were carried to Hailes where his stepmother, Sanchia, had already been laid to rest: the place of burial was said to be near the high altar. W. St Clair Baddeley, excavating at Hailes in 1899, wrote:

I opened up the front of the high altar and two foot down I came across Early English fragments of canopy work, one bit of lead coffin, iron clamping and fragments of several members of bone, a fleur de lys tile and one of an eagle.[8]

A furnace was placed very near this spot at the Dissolution (a small mound remains there still) and it is impossible to know whether any of these fragments should be associated with Henry's burial. The Hailes chronicler sadly recorded an epitaph: 'The sword of the accursed stock of Simon pierced his Heart, Oh Queen of Heaven intercede for Him.'

The baronial wars brought much misery to Richard and drew him away from his German kingdom. He had been approached by a group of German magnates in 1257 under the leadership of the Archbishop of Cologne who wished to elect him as King of the Romans. Their choice, according to Matthew Paris, was 'on account of his fidelity, firmness and wisdom' but, he adds darkly, also 'on account of his wealth'. Richard's decision to accept may have been after some hesitation for, while he must have known that loyalty to his brother left little scope for his own ambitions at home, Henry was, nevertheless, likely to find himself in difficulties again and to call once more for help. It is possible that Sanchia wished to be crowned queen like her sisters and Richard must have wished for an opportunity to prove himself in matters of government.

Richard and his queen were crowned at Aachen in 1257 by the

Archbishop of Cologne. Some accounts state that the Earl brought his own regalia.[9] Despite generous grants of charters to German cities and other institutions Richard's grasp of his new kingdom had been weak. His election had not been unanimous and before long his brother called him home in the wars of de Montfort. Sanchia died all too soon, on 5 November 1261 at Richard's palace at Berkhampstead, and her body was brought to Hailes for burial. Richard married for the third time, choosing Beatrix, a German wife, but his absences in England, stories of his ignominious part in the Battle of Lewes[10] and his later imprisonment lowered his prestige and weakened his position. He returned like a ghost to his German kingdom. It is clear that when he had time and opportunity to deal with his affairs there he was not lacking in administrative ability.

The death of his cherished son, Henry, had undoubtedly been a mortal blow. His world had gone sour. He had lived a hectic life, travelled far, been much involved in affairs of state and diplomacy but he lived to see his name tarnished, his heir cruelly murdered by his nephews; and, according to Matthew Paris, he had never enjoyed robust health. On 13 December 1271 he suffered a stroke in his Berkhampstead home which paralysed his right side and took away his power of speech.

Richard lingered until the spring and died on 2 April 1272 at the age of sixty-three. His heart was buried in the church of the Friars Minor at Oxford of whom he was a patron: his young bride was later buried in the same place.[11] Richard's bones were carried to Hailes for honourable burial. He was buried in the traditional founder's place, on the north side of the chancel near the high altar, presumably next to Sanchia and not far from the murdered Henry. Richard's arms as Earl of Cornwall and King of the Romans, together with the arms associated with Sanchia, probably marked the area of the burial. A surviving tiled pavement in the north choir aisle was lifted in 1980 but the details were carefully recorded in a plan which is now in the museum. Of Richard's tomb nothing identifiable remains. Fragments of an effigy of an armed man have been found but cannot be certainly identified. It is likely that Richard's tomb was similar to those of Aylmer of Valence or Edmund Crouchback at Westminster, or the near contemporary tabernacle tombs in Tewkesbury Abbey.

The Hailes chronicle in its epitaph for its founder described him as 'offspring of the King of England, formerly Count of Poitou and Earl of Cornwall. Later honoured with the golden crown of Charlemagne bearing as his arms on his shield the eagle and the lion rampant.' These arms may well have been used to decorate his tomb, possibly with the accolade of the Hailes chronicler: 'pre-eminent amongst kings of all races for his moderation, worldly riches, wisdom, modesty, a man of probity all his days'.

Richard's surviving son, Edmund, who had been hastily called home after his brother's murder, now took the title of Earl of Cornwall and became the abbey's patron and benefactor. It was Edmund who gave Hailes the famous relic which drew pilgrims to the abbey through the centuries, and which forms the subject of Chapter Three.

2. THE FOUNDATION AND BUILDING OF THE MONASTERY

Hailes Abbey received its foundation charter in 1246 and was ready for dedication by 1251. The dates are significant for the period of building: Richard's magnificent new abbey coincided with an outburst of building activity in England and abroad. His royal brother was rebuilding Westminster Abbey[1] and his brother-in-law, King Louis of France, was supervising the creation of La Sainte Chapelle, while much work was in hand at Notre Dame. The church at Tintern, the choir at Southwell, the presbytery of Lincoln and Ely were among other works in progress. There was much to inspire Richard's enterprise at Hailes.

Vows made in time of danger and faithfully fulfilled were common in the middle ages. Although Matthew Paris tells the story of Earl Richard's near shipwreck, the two chronicles written by monks of his abbey make no mention of the incident. The words of the foundation charter of Hailes, dated 16 June 1246, are explicit with regard to details: the founder, his reasons, the Order of monks, the site, the grants and privilege which comprised the endowment are all there.

To all sons of Holy Mother Church to whom this present writing shall come, Richard, Earl of Cornwall [sends] greetings in the Lord. Let it be known that we, in honour of Almighty God and the Glorious Virgin Mary and All Saints for the good of our Soul, the Souls of our predecessors and successors, have founded a certain abbey of the Cistercian Order in the manor of Hailes, which we have received by gift of Henry, King of England, our brother.

The choice of the Cistercian Order (the White Monks) may have owed something to the popularity of the Order at the time. The chronicler of Waverley Abbey, Surrey (the first Cistercian foundation in England, 1128) wrote that 'guided by Divine inspiration, taking the Cistercian Order as a model of excellence before all others [Richard] chose it for his new monastery at Hailes'.

Richard, by the standards of his time a religious man, was certainly a patron of the Cistercian abbey of Pontigny where he made pilgrimage to the shrine of the English saint, St Edmund Rich. The Earl spent considerable sums embellishing that shrine and named his second son after the saint. In 1246, Beaulieu Abbey, founded by his father King John, was solemnly dedicated in the presence of the King, Queen, Richard with his family and a great concourse of clergy and nobles. Beaulieu was a daughter house of the abbey of Cîteaux in Burgundy, which had given its name to the Order. From his father's abbey, Richard took twenty monks and ten lay brothers[2] (*conversi*) to create his daughter house at Hailes. It is possible too that the number of other Orders in the region around Hailes also dictated his choice to some extent.[3]

The site at Hailes was in many ways highly suitable for Cistercian settlement. It was a secluded hamlet sheltered by the wooded slopes of the Cotswold escarpment, opening out to the Vale of Evesham and the Severn Valley to the west and screened by an intervening hill from the nearby and long-established Winchcombe Abbey.

Beaulieu Abbey had taken some forty-two years to complete — 'by no means an old lady' said the writer of the evocative description of the scene as the founding fathers prepared to leave the mother house of Beaulieu, led by Prior Jordan who was to be the first Abbot of Hailes. The chronicler makes much use of the symbolism of his name. After a final meal in the *frater*, where 'the sound of weeping was more often heard than rejoicing', the party of thirty received a solemn blessing and, in procession behind an uplifted cross, made their way to the boundaries of Beaulieu to start their journey to the unknown. Richard and Henry with a large entourage were there to witness their departure.

The chronicler of Hailes makes an allegory of the rigours and bleakness of this colonising enterprise. The journey was made in six stages 'just as Heaven and earth were completed in the space of six days'. The monks broke their journey at Harford, Romsey, Andover, Coxwell and Salperton.[4] Richard had apparently provided an escort for their safety and saw that they had ample provisions. While those in the mother house 'wept like Rachel for her children and would not be comforted', the pioneers 'like John the Baptist in the wilderness' crossed the open country mainly on Beaulieu estates. Suitably, on 23 June, the Eve of John the Baptist's Day, they reached Hailes. Their first sight of Hailes appears to have filled them with dismay for, according to the chronicler, 'each and everyone seeing the roughness of the terrain might well have said "how awful is this place" wondering how from such unpromising beginnings might grow a noble monastery'. The new arrivals might have comforted themselves by reflecting on the words of St Bernard, their great saint, 'Believe one who has tried it, you will find among woods something you will never find in books. Stones and trees will teach you letters you could never learn from masters in the Schools.'

At Hailes there was sufficient flat land for the essential monastic buildings, the fertile soil was suitable for arable farming and orchards, and the Cotswold uplands excellent as sheep pasture. Moreover, there were numerous quarries of honey-coloured limestone in the area to supply the demands of buildings as extensive as those Richard demanded. There was timber in plenty for domestic use and the Forest of Dean, not too distant, afforded great oaks for constructional purposes. The area was well watered by springs and streams from the hills, ready to work mills and workshops essential in a Cistercian abbey where the monks were to survive by their labours. 'Our monasteries,' said the statues of the Order, 'are not to be built in cities, castles or villages but in places remote from the conversation of men'.

Within five years of their arrival, by November 1251, 'a fine church, adequate dormitory, dignified *frater* and a large spacious cloister walk with adjoining buildings' was erected ready for dedication. The new monastery took its name from the manor. The Hailes chronicler derived the name from the Old English word meaning healthy.[5] He vigorously supported his view from the evidence of the first seven years of the abbey during which, despite all hardships and dangers, there was no sickness and no death.

Cistercian statutes insisted that temporary accommodation had to be provided so that, immediately on arrival, a new community could take up the daily round of services. According to the chronicle, the monks arriving in June 1246 'set up their tents at Hailes mill'.[6] Perhaps the little parish church, already a century old, was used for services. The villagers who, with their mill, are recorded in Domesday had probably been moved to nearby Didbrook where a new church was built for them by 1257.[7] 'They have built their monasteries in deserted or woodland places,' wrote the Benedictine, Orderic Vitalis. The satirical writer, Walter Map, put it differently: 'desert places do they assuredly either find — or make'.

13th-century boss showing Christ as a spiritual Samson rending the lion's jaw

Early Cistercians did much of their own building and the Order was renowned for its pioneering efforts in the design of conduits, drains and watermills in particular. Surviving remains are evidence of the enduring quality of Cistercian building skills. (Water still flows through the great drain at Hailes after seven-and-a-half centuries.) Hailes, however, was a late foundation with a wealthy owner ready to spend generously. The monks doubtless provided assistance and the chronicler implies that Richard supplied workmen of his own in the early stages. He may have called in masons and carpenters who had worked on his castles. The villagers of Didbrook presumably found work clearing the site, and any skilled carpenters or masons in the community would have been recruited. There is record of considerable building activity at Evesham, Gloucester, Pershore and Tewkesbury in this period, so that travelling masons and carpenters could have been hired easily. The Earl may also have employed men who had gained experience at Westminster: the quality of surviving stone work and tiles at Hailes is evidence that expert masons, sculptors and tilers were used. The beautiful roof bosses now on display in the museum (where some may be seen at close quarters) are of outstanding quality, deeply undercut with gracefully carved petals, leaves and tendrils. The most impressive is that of Christ as a spiritual Samson engaged in a struggle with a lion.[8]

In charge of the entire building operation, according to medieval practice, was the *cementarius*, the name given to the medieval working architect (from the Latin *cementum*, stone). The abbey chronicle indicates that he was a monk, 'Brother John the *cementarius*'.[9] John was approaching his seventieth year when, at a Rogationtide sometime before the dedication service in 1251, he was introduced to Earl Richard. The chronicle sees this as confirmation of the healthiness of the site. It is possible that Brother John had come with the pioneering party from Beaulieu: features of the earliest arches of the east cloister walk, such as the processional doorway and the arched recesses of the north cloister wall, can be compared with details of the mother house. The fact that the building of the abbey coincided with the period of the Earl's greatest prosperity, before his fortune was dissipated in his German kingdom, may explain the speed with which it was build. Most medieval buildings reveal the ebb and flow of the fortunes of their patrons, for example, Beaulieu after the death of King John, or Tewkesbury, which suffered from the fluctuating fortunes of the Despensers.

An army of workmen must have been needed on the site before building could begin: tree fellers, sawyers, scaffolders, lime burners, mortarmakers, tool sharpeners, carters and carriers of every kind.[10] Stone had to be selected, dressed and prepared in the quarries above Hailes. Lanes and tracks needed to be cleared and firmed, and bridges built or strengthened to carry heavy loads. Once the site had been cleared and rammed firm, the plan would have been pegged out and the foundations checked. Hailes was built on clay and the continuous platform of the choir arcade is still visible.

Contemporary manuscripts bring the scene alive. In the centre of activity is the *cementarius*, usually distinguished by his cap and gown, keeping a watchful eye on the whole scene. Around him are scaffolding of ropes, windlasses, cranes, pulleys, ropes attached to beams raising prepared stones, wooden frames (around which arches were constructed), hurdles with poles attached, like litters, for carrying dressed stone, and whetstones for sharpening tools. In the background would be the master mason's tracing hut, where plans were drawn on board, slate, plaster or, more rarely because of expense, on linen or parchment.[11]

No Fabric Rolls survive for the building of Hailes as they do for Westminster or Vale Royal (founded by Richard's nephew Edward I), but there is evidence of the cost. Matthew Paris, indefatigable as ever in search for facts for his chronicle, asked the question for us after the dedication ceremony, at which he was apparently present:

When I, Matthew Paris, desirous to be informed upon the matter, in order that I might not insert falsities in this book, the earl with unhesitating certainty informed me that when all expenses were reckoned he had laid out ten thousand marks in the building of that church; adding this remarkable and praise-worthy speech: 'would that it had pleased God that I had expended all that I have laid out in the castle at Wallingford in as wise and salutary a manner!'

The Hailes chronicle noted 'the cost to that noble man, Richard Earl of Cornwall, Founder of this place was 8000 marks[12] for the work'. The Annals of Waverley recorded that Richard gave the monks 1000 marks to purchase lands or build houses, and the King settled on them a yearly rent of £20. (It is not certain that this payment was maintained.) The building was of the local oolite limestone, set off with details in pillars and sculpture in blue lias slate. The surviving capitals which flank the *frater* door give some idea of the delicate stiff-leaf foliage achieved in this medium. Fragments of colour reveal that the interior was whitened and picked out with red outlining to suggest strong joints, while doors were also outlined in red. Examples of this can still be seen in one of the windows in the undercroft, and on the roof of one of the wall recesses in the north cloister. Further examples may be seen in the cloister museum.

13th-century vaulting bosses found in the Chapter House, now in the Abbey Museum

15th-century bosses found in the Chapter House

In 1246, right at the beginning of the work, King Henry gave forty oaks from the Forest of Dean 'for some work which Richard of Cornwall is about to found in the manor of Hailes'. The following year he presented another sixty oaks. In 1251, when the work was nearing completion, more oaks were required for the choir stalls, obviously in preparation for the dedication service in November of that year. In 1252, twenty more oaks were ordered by the king to be delivered for the completion of the dormitory.[13] Iron from Gloucester, to make tie bars, was purchased for Westminster (four tons at four shillings a cwt) between 1252 and 1253, so it seems probable that Hailes drew from the same source.

The monks had an early gift for their library shelves. A surviving manuscript records that in 1248: 'The Lord Abbot and convent of Caerleon gave to the convent of Hailes at the instance of the Lord Richard, Earl of Cornwall, distinguished founder of that house and brother of the Lord Henry, king of England' a 12th-century copy of the *Homilies of St Gregory*. It must have been a sacrifice for the little Welsh community.

The abbey church, dedicated in 1251, was of the traditional cruciform plan with three chapels in each transept, like Beaulieu, but, whereas the mother church ended in an eastern apse with an ambulatory, Hailes at this stage had a straight east wall flanked by two turrets with spiral staircases. The foundations are still visible.

While the walls were steadily rising and the royal oaks were being trundled across the shire, it is possible that the conversation of the workmen at Hailes was on the traditional English subject, the weather. According to Matthew Paris

1246   While the laborious seasons of July and August were occupying farmers an unprecedented and destructive storm and thunder which lasted an entire day and night terrified the whole length and breadth of England and many men and cattle were killed by lightning. About the same time Earl Richard founded a house for the Cistercian Order in a favourable situation not far from Winchcombe.

1247   There was such protracted inclemency of the weather and an unseasonable and wintery roughness, disturbed and cold and rainy that the husbandmen and gardeners complained that spring by a backward movement was changed to winter.

1248   The temperature of winter was entirely changed to that of spring so that neither snow nor frost covered the face of the earth for two days together. Trees might be seen shooting in February, and the birds singing and sporting as if in April.

On 5 November, 1251, a Sunday, the church at Hailes was dedicated. Matthew Paris sets the scene:

There was present the Earl Richard, the King and Queen with the Lord Edward, their noble first born. There were thirteen bishops at the church and many others both abbots and priors of various orders and over and above that, the great men of England, earls, barons and other nobles who came to the said monastery on the same day.

The Hailes chronicler added 'with a host of lesser folk beyond count', and explained that 'the thirteen bishops each stood next to an altar which he consecrated in the name of Jesus and the twelve apostles'. The number of altars here suggests that there were chapels against the east wall behind the altar, reached by an ambulatory. The Bishop of Lincoln, the great Robert Grosseteste, said Mass at the high altar. Generous indulgences were awarded by each bishop, making in all a total of 'five hundred days in relaxation for those who gave offerings'. The church was dedicated, as all Cistercian monasteries were, to the Virgin Mary, and also to the Holy Trinity and All Saints.

After the solemnities there was a splendid feast. Matthew tells us:

The nobles feasted sumptuously in company with the bishops and others who ate meat while the Religious took their places and refreshed themselves with large quantities of fish of various kinds. There were also present three hundred soldiers.

Excavations on the site of the misericord[14] for sick monks at Westminster have uncovered evidence for more than twenty different kinds of fish including sturgeon and also wildfowl. Matthew concludes his account of the celebrations at Hailes: 'Indeed if I were to describe in full the grandeur of that solemn and festive occasion I should be said to have exceeded the bounds of truth.'

The great concourse at Hailes on this occasion must have given Richard of Cornwall considerable satisfaction. The numbers would have provided a very real catering problem. If, as seems likely, the abbey *frater* was in use this was the greatest number of people ever at table there as the average number of monks at Hailes appears to have been twenty-two! We know that in 1299, when Edward I visited the monastery, Peter the Spicer, apothecary to Queen

Margaret, was in attendance for in his expense account he includes the cost of transport to Hailes. After such celebrations as those in 1251 it is likely that someone like Peter would have been kept busy!

Only six years after these events Richard and Sanchia left England for their joint coronation as King and Queen of the Romans in another glittering ceremony at Aachen.[15] In their absence the monks soon found themselves in financial difficulties.

Sanchia was present with Richard at the Hailes consecration but the place must have had unhappy associations for her. The abbey chronicle records that 'Richard, son of Richard, Earl of Cornwall, whom Sanchia had borne him, died and was buried at Grove Mill near Hailes in 1246'. The chronicle adds that when the building was completed he was removed to Hailes where he was honourably buried. It is just possible that the curious small coffin stone in Didbrook churchyard may have marked his temporary place of burial. It shows a small head under a gabled canopy with a cross. If the chronicle entry is correct Sanchia and Richard were there when the monks arrived from Beaulieu, or soon after.

Sanchia was the next casualty. In 1261, only a decade after the dedication, her body was brought in a solemn cortège, accompanied by Boniface, Archbishop of Canterbury, and Peter of Savoy (both relations) from Berkhampstead to Hailes. Richard was not present at the funeral but he left money for a chaplain to pray daily for her soul in the Chapel of St John in the Tower of London. The King made similar provision. Sanchia left her heart to Cirencester Abbey, with £100.[16] Her family arms, with the eagle for the German kingdom, are thickly scattered on the tiles near her presumed place of burial at Hailes.

Ten years later the remains of Henry, her stepson, were brought to Hailes, to be followed a year later by those of Richard. As patron, Richard and his family were entitled to burial within the abbey church so that they might lie assured of the prayers of the community.

It was left to Sanchia's son, Edmund, to complete the last major building programme at Hailes: a beautiful chevet, or crown, of five chapels with the shrine of the Holy Blood set like a jewel in the centre. The building of this chevet, clearly influenced by French architecture (Westminster has a similar feature and it appears in a modified form at Tewkesbury), altered the plain square end of the abbey church. It is not clear when the 'new work' (or new church as

Ground plan of the chevet from the north-east, showing the base of the shrine and its encircling pillars. Cloister arches visible in the background.

it is variously called in the chronicles) began. Edmund had obtained the relic of the Holy Blood in 1265 but did not bring it to Hailes until 1270. It was probably placed in a safe position until the work was competed sometime before 1277, when the Bishop of Worcester[17] dedicated the shrine on the Thursday after Trinity. In the early 16th-century a monk of Hailes wrote:

He built a chapel there with five altars about
upon them he spared no expense
For they be royal enough within, without
A shrine he made also, a noble and rich,
of gold and silver and precious stones.
In England there were few it like,
For it was ordered for the very thing.
And Geoffrey Gifford, Bishop of Worcester
He hallowed that place better.

Edmund died at Ashridge in October 1300.[18] His heart and intestines were buried there but his bones were brought to Winchcombe Abbey where Hailes monks stood watch until the funeral cortège could proceed to Hailes.[19] The ceremony did not take place until April 1301. The delay may have been caused by the need to wait for the King, Edmund's cousin, to be free to attend. Edward 1 and his queen accompanied the funeral procession from Winchcombe along the still-existing footpath through Rowley meadow and into the Salt Way. The service was conducted by the Archbishop of Canterbury and the Bishops of Exeter, Chester and Hereford. Sixteen abbots and many priests attended with hosts of religious. The site of Edmund's tomb in the abbey is not known: as patron and son of the founder he would have had a place of honour near the high altar. Fragments of a military effigy found there could have belonged to the tombs of Richard, Henry or Edmund.

Building on a small scale continued at Hailes, presumably when money was available. Edmund died a very wealthy man, and may well have remembered the abbey where his mother, father and brothers were buried and where he would lie.[20]

In 1292, 'the infirmary and adjoining buildings were begun on the morrow of the Annunciation of the Blessed Virgin, a Tuesday', the Hailes chronicler records. The next year finishing touches were put to these buildings, for King Edward granted 'a licence to crenellate some chambers newly constructed in the abbey'. There was a severe storm on 19 July, with thunder and lightning; many men and cattle were killed, including a man who died near Hailes.

The last recorded building was in 1299 when, on 22 June, work was begun on an ox-house which was completed in the same year.

By the 15th-century, the abbey buildings were, as we shall see, in a state of dilapidation and a programme of rebuilding began, probably under Abbot Whitchurch. The new cloisters, of which there is evidence today, belong to this period, and the Abbot's house, in the west range, was greatly improved.

3. THE HOLY BLOOD

By God's precious heart and Passion, by God's nails
And by the Blood of Christ that is in Hailes. *Chaucer, The Pardoner's Tale.*

At the Blood of Hayles
Where Pylgrymes paynes right much avayles. *John Heywood.*

Grant us oft tymes while on earth we shall tarry
To come to Hayles with most sober mode
To see and visit the precious portion of His Blood
Which dropped from the wound that was full wide
Made with the spear of Longinus in His side. *'A monk of Hailes', 16th century*

One of the chronicles of Hailes tells the story of the Holy Blood and how it came to the abbey, and there is a 'Little Treatise on Divers Miracles which God has shewed for the portion of His Precious Blood in Hayles' of the 16th century, written probably by a monk of the abbey. From these two sources it is possible to know how medieval pilgrims viewed the relic, and what they were told about it.

When Richard of Cornwall became King of the Romans his son, Edmund, accompanied him into Germany with Sanchia his mother. The young Prince struck up a friendship with Roger, son of Sir Wariner of Boyland (or Doyland?) who was custodian of Trevelyan's castle, where the imperial regalia was housed with other jewels and relics. These attracted Edmund's attention but, as he played, one object in particular stood out. This was plated with gold, clasped with a golden chain and secured on all sides with locks. When Edmund asked what it was that was so closely guarded, he was told that it was a relic containing the Blood of Christ and that it was hung around the neck of the Emperor when he was anointed, after the ceremony of election.

Edmund begged Roger to intercede with his father so that he might be given a portion of the Blood. To this the custodian eventually agreed. A little of the Blood was poured into a container and Edmund took it back to England. For a time he kept the precious relic at the castle at Wallingford until he decided that part of it should be given to his father's monastery of Hailes, where his mother was buried. The Hailes chronicle gives 1267 as the date when

Edmund acquired the Holy Blood, which means that he would have been seventeen at the time of the incident, scarcely the age to be playing in the German castle as the story suggests!

According to the 'Little Treatise', when Christ was hanging on the Cross a certain Jew, a convert to Christianity, came secretly to the place, bearing with him a small vessel in which he collected some of the Blood from Christ's side. The Jews, learning what had taken place, imprisoned him, with his precious relic, in a stone house outside the city and mockingly left him there with the vessel of Blood as his only sustenance. There he remained for forty-two years, sustained only by the Blood until the Emperors Titus and Vespasian besieged Jerusalem and reduced it to ruins. As they were returning home, the Emperors saw the little house and enquired what it was. They were told the story of the believing Jew and his fate and at once broke into the prison, and found the Jew still alive, the Vessel of Blood still in his lap. In fear and wonderment they questioned him and, hearing the story, they demanded that he give them the relic. When he refused they seized the vessel. At once, the Jew 'lost both syght and speeche and fell in powder as dead as stone'.

The 'Little Treatise' continues: 'as it is written in the Gospel, where thy treasure is there is thy heart also'. So the Jew died but was at once received in Heaven. The victorious leaders returned to Rome bearing with them the Holy Blood, with another relic said to be the skin of the circumcision. The relics were placed in the Temple of Peace in Rome where they remained until the Emperor Charlemagne entered the city and took part of the Blood back to Germany. It was deposited in Trevelyan's castle where Edmund had found it and was greatly venerated there.

A more credible version of Edmund's acquisition of the relic suggests that he purchased it from Count Florenz V of Holland, after it had been brought into Europe by his predecessor, Count William II, with a seal of authenticity from the Patriarch of Jerusalem later Pope Urban IV (1261-4). The latter was a Cistercian monk, so the Hailes monks would have reason to accept this version. There was no mention of any such documentation at the Dissolution.

Edmund spent the night of 12 September 1270 at Winchcombe Abbey and, on the following day, Holy Rood Day, the relic was borne with great reverence to Hailes. The procession made its way along Puckpit Lane and Rowley Meadow, where Abbot Walter and the Hailes monks met it. A great throng of people crowded along the route. A halt was made in the meadow, and a canopy of cloth of gold was erected over an altar so that the sacred relic could be displayed for veneration. Abbot Walter then preached a sermon expounding the story of the Holy Blood while onlookers, laughing with joy, 'crept on their knees'.[1] The procession then re-formed, and black and white robed monks from the two monasteries walked together to the abbey church, Edmund holding the sacred relic.[2]

In the church the monks of Winchcombe sat on one side of the choir, the monks of Hailes on the other, while Edmund offered the relic at the high altar. The ceremony over, the Winchcombe monks returned home. Their old shrine to St Kenelm was to be overshadowed by the one erected at Hailes.

The foundation platform of the shrine still remains, just off the centre of the chevet. It is not known exactly what form the shrine took, but it is presumed to have been a small ark-like structure similar perhaps to the surviving shrines at Westminster or St Albans, or the descriptions of Becket's shrine at Canterbury, although it is unlikely to have rivalled the latter in splendour.[3]

The relic itself was described at the Dissolution as being contained in a round 'beryl, very securely stopped and ornamented and bound round with silver'. The seal of the Confraternity of Hailes shows such a bottle from which projects the head of a cross. This may represent the gold cross, with an enamel base, containing a fragment of the True Cross, which Edmund gave to the abbey.[4]

The chapel of the shrine, behind the high altar, can be imagined from the evidence of the pillar bases (only one of which is original) which half encircle the shrine. It has been suggested that the west tower arch and west window at Teddington church may have come from this part of Hailes after the Dissolution.

Pilgrims descending the Salt Way would have caught their first sight of the monastery from above and excitement must have grown when, after entering through the main gate and crossing the great court, they came near the church. They may have entered the church by the north transept and passed along the tiled path of the north choir aisle, pausing to marvel at the tombs of Richard and Sanchia before they passed into the chevet. (A walk round the choir of Tewkesbury today, with the tombs of its medieval patrons clustered around the high altar, gives an idea of the scene.) The five polygonal chapels, each with its own altar and richly tiled floors, stood on the left hand side, while the chapel of the shrine was on their right. As the guardian of the shrine revealed the relic and told its story, there must have been many wide-eyed pilgrims. Candlelight[5] gleaming on the rich colour of the glazed and decorated floor tiles, and light from the windows of the chevet, will have added to the wonder of the moment and made the scene unforgettable for those who had travelled far.

The abbey claimed many miracles for its relics:

... God himself showed with many miracles
For the precious portion of His Blood that is in Hailes
The number of whom no man knoweth but God himself alone
For they be so renewed and increase daily

So wrote the 16th-century author of the 'Little Treatise'. He relates four miracles. The first is of a Lollard priest in Shropshire who, one Easter, tried to dissuade his parishioners from a proposed pilgrimage to see the Holy Blood, assuring them that it would do them no good. The villagers however, unconvinced, set out before dawn, leaving the priest behind. As he uncovered the chalice at Mass 'after the Pater Noster' he saw 'in dread and wonder' that the wine was 'boiling to the very brink'. Hastily repenting his unbelief the priest set out from Hailes immediately after dinner and, walking rapidly, caught up with his parishioners at Worcester and became a devout and humble member of their fellowship.

The second miracle moves to Derbyshire and concerns another unbelieving priest who discouraged pilgrims he met in a hostelry for travellers, until one day as he was singing divine service he found the words of his service book obscured by a sprinkling of blood. Trembling and awestruck he turned the book around, but the writing remained unreadable. Then his heart turned cold and he vowed to mend his ways and go on pilgrimage to Hailes, shirtless and barefooted. There, with his parishioners as witnesses, 'he confessed his sins and, kneeling on the stones, he honoured the Blood'.

The third tale concerned a baker from Stone (Stow?) who, with his wife and children, set off with a cart according to custom, to spend the period from Whitsun to Corpus Christi selling to pilgrims. On the Monday after the Feast of Corpus Christi they packed up their things, stacked unsold goods in the cart and put the children on top and set off for home. As they were ascending Pyseley Hill, his wife remonstrated with him that during the fifteen days they had been at Hailes they had not once done honour to the Holy Blood. Her husband saw the point and, tying up the cart with the three children on top, the parents retraced their steps and entered the church to pray. In their absence 'a wicked sprite' frightened the horses which bolted in terror over the uneven ground, pitted with limeburners' pits and stone quarries. The cart, its axles broken, was smashed to bits but miraculously the children were unharmed. The grateful parents returned once more to the shrine, this time to give thanks.

The last and most elaborate story was likened to the miraculous delivery of St Peter from prison. Two English merchants, John Marshall and Robert Johns, from Webley in Lincolnshire, were captured at sea and imprisoned in Mont St Michel. John, who knew his psalms by heart, besought God's help. One night he was awakened by a bright light and heard a voice telling him to go to the Blood. John thought it must be an hallucination but after a month was finally convinced. On Christmas Eve, the voice told him to trust in God's grace; John accordingly woke his companion to find their chains had fallen off and the prison gates were open. They passed out unhindered through the castle gates and, the tide having ebbed, crossed safely to the mainland where they found a ship and sailed to Wales. They told their story, inquired about the Blood and were directed to Our Lady's monastery of Hailes. They came thither and swore on the Gospel that their story was true. The monks 'sang the Te Deum full solemnly and well, from beginning to end' and, after walking in procession, the two travellers left their lighted tapers and generous offerings at the shrine.

The story of the captured merchants imprisoned in France must have struck a chord in the hearts of dealers who came to Hailes to buy the monastery's wool, and knew the danger of the Channel, especially during the wars with France.

Pilgrims flocked to the shrine during the later Middle Ages: Chaucer mentions the Holy Blood. Among those who we know came to Hailes on pilgrimage was the redoubtable Margery Kemp from Lynn who, on her return from Compostella via Bristol, 'went forth to the Blood of Hailes and there she was shriven with loud cries and boisterous weeping. Then the religious men had her in among them and made great cheer save they swore many and great oaths and horrible. She rebuked them after the Gospel and thereof they had great wonder.'

The year was 1417 when the fortunes of the abbey were very low. The monks probably welcomed the opportunity to hear about the great shrine at Compostella, enough to ignore statutes forbidding lay folk in the cloister, let alone a woman. Margery's characteristic bluntness must have made them realise that perhaps there was sense in that prohibition but, as Margery noted, 'some were right well pleased'. Could it have been Margery, coming from East Anglia, who lost the pilgrim token from Bury St Edmunds (discovered early in this century) which is now at the museum at Bury? No Hailes tokens have been found.

A series of papal indulgences in the 15th century indicates the poor state of the monastery in the period, and the part pilgrims were encouraged to take by way of generous offering to help restore the fabric. Pope John XXIII (deposed 1415) gave Abbot Henley power to find two confessors to hear confessions of pilgrims and grant them absolution. Similar privileges were granted to brothers and sisters of the Confraternity of Hailes, whose seal with a Latin inscription, 'seal of the Fraternity of the monastery of the Blessed Mary of Hayles', has survived. Pictured on the seal is a monk holding the flask of Holy Blood with a cross issuing from the neck of the bottle. A document in the abbey museum, issued to Lord Charles Herbert of Raglan[6] in 1509, indicates the nature of the Confraternity. It grants to him and his wife:

by virtue of Christ and His most precious Blood full participation in all spiritual benefits of the Order. (Canonical Hours, Masses, Prayers, fasts, vigils, penances, scourages, abstinences, acts of mercy, hospitality and labours of all services of Divine worship.)

Pope John's privileges conclude the grant:

a suitable confessor whom you choose will grant and be empowered to grant and impart to you full remission of all your sins of which in life and on the point of death you have repented, as for all the brethren, sisters and friends and more especially benefactors of our monastery.

Edward Stafford, Duke of Buckingham,[7] is reputed to have come to Hailes on pilgrimage before his execution and Prior More, the rather worldly Benedictine from Worcester, recorded in his Account

British Museum

Seal of the Confraternity of Hailes

Book that, in 1530, he spent: '2s. 4d. on riding to Hayles from Cropthorne on pilgrimage'. As late as 1533 Hugh Latimer wrote: 'I dwell within a mile of the Foss Way and you would wonder how they come by flocks out of the West country to Our Lady of Worcester but chiefly to the Blood of Hailes which they believe the very sight of it puts them in a state of salvation'.

But there were doubters. There had probably always been those who found it difficult to accept the stories about the relic. The Hailes chronicle prefaces its account of the young Edmund in Trevelyan's castle with a comment on those who 'not knowing past events adhere to false opinions' about the genuineness of the relic. It does not give the story of the believing Jew but takes up the narrative with the relic's appearance among Charlemagne's regalia. The 16th-century account not only tells stories of those who doubted the relic but also specifically refers to the mistrusting nature of men and asks: 'Why is it more against men's wit to believe that

Christ's Blood is in Hailes than on the Circumcision that is in Rome?', and goes on to admit 'much of the people is oft in doubt of this precious Blood that is in Hayles'.

There were certainly doubters towards the end of the abbey's history. In 1509 a Roger Brown of Coventry was accused of heresy because he thought 'men should worship Almighty God not the image of Our Lady of Walsingham nor the Holy Blood of Hailes'. A vicar of Windrush was reputed to have regretted that he had wasted money on Our Lady of Worcester and the Blood of Hailes. He declared that he had 'done as an ill husbandman that ploughed his land and sowed nothing to the purpose, for he had worshipped man's handiwork and cast away his money'.

In the late days of the monastery a William Thomas maintained that two monks killed a duck every Saturday and with it renewed the Blood as they themselves confessed, not only in secret, but also openly before an approving audience! The Last Abbot, Stephen Sagar, took pains to refute this rumour, protesting in a letter to Thomas Cromwell that, to his knowledge, the relic was in its original condition. He cited an eighty-year-old guardian of the shrine who would confirm this. William Thomas described the Blood as contained in a crystal glass as thick as a bowl on one side and thin as a glass on the other. Camden supported the story asserting that the Blood was only liquefied to penitents when the thinner side of the glass was turned towards them.[8]

However, the shrine was receiving ten pounds a year in offerings as late as 1534, less than the shrines at Walsingham and Canterbury but more than the average, and it certainly outshone that at Winchcombe.[9]

Sagar eventually asked permission to dispose of 'that feigned relic' and, in November 1539, Bishop Hilsey of Rochester declared it to be a forgery.

Wonder-working shrines and relics were not usually found in Cistercian monasteries because of the disruptive influence of pilgrims invading the precincts. It is ironic that Hailes needed the income derived from pilgrims to keep its fabric in repair.

4. THE EARLY YEARS OF THE MONASTERY

When the ceremony of dedication was over in November 1251, the monks were left to face the winter in buildings not yet fully completed and without some essential farming materials. Between 1251 and the dedication of the 'new work' of the chevet in 1277, Richard, Sanchia, her infant son and Prince Henry were all, by exercise of founder's privileges, buried in the abbey church so that they could benefit from the daily routine of prayer and service. (Cistercian statutes stated that none should be buried in the greater churches but kings, queens and bishops.[1]) The work of completing the monastic buildings, and the inevitable disturbance of these burials at Hailes with the setting of tiled pavements (bearing arms associated with their families) must have caused difficulties for the monks who were trying to establish a settled routine in a new, as yet uncompleted, abbey.

Shortage of money must also have presented a problem for the monks. The founder, so generous in paying for the initial building programme, was now preoccupied by affairs of state: the growing unrest between King and barons (vividly described by Matthew Paris), the Battles of Lewes (1264) and Evesham (1265), and Richard's election to the German throne meant that he had little time or money to spend on the new monastery. Richard did return to the abbey, on Palm Sunday 1258, during one of his visits from Germany, with a great concourse of people including Walter Cantelupe, Bishop of Worcester.[2] Edmund had, by this date, obtained the Holy Blood and it is conceivable that he participated in the plans for the new chevet to house the shrine. His initial endowment of the abbey had been generous and included the manor of Hailes with 'rents in woods, meadows, plains, pastures, watermills, ponds, fishponds, paths and ways, as well as the customary services of freeman and villeins'. He also gave the advowson of the little parish church, which soon came into the abbey's hands, and £1000 to be expended in land or buildings. The King gave a yearly rent and twenty marks. The nearby manor of Pinnockshire probably came to the abbey within a decade.

It has been suggested that the abbey site may have covered some fifty acres in all, the boundaries reaching to the Salt Way on the south and west and possibly to the churchyard on the north.[3] The engraving by Kip of the early 18th century would appear to confirm this. The outer court of the abbey is now meadow. The task of organising the work of the community with its agricultural basis

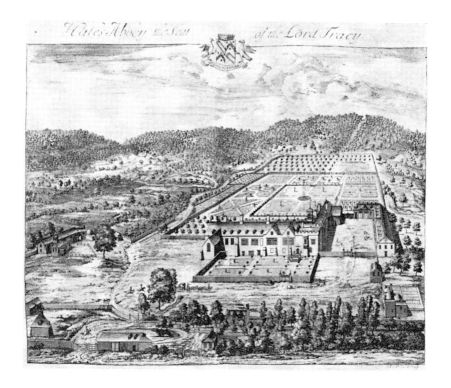

The west range of the cloister when it was the home of the Tracy family. View by Kip, c. 1712

must have seemed a formidable problem without the need to complete the buildings in the absence of a regular income. The Cistercians have been described as the greatest boon to agriculture that England ever received for it was a fundamental principle that they should live by their labour, cultivating the soil and breeding cattle, pigs and sheep. The impressive 13th-century account book of the mother house at Beaulieu gives a vivid picture of the activities of an established Cistercian house, revealing the duties of a host of officials: infirmarian, forester, farrier, cellarer, baker, hospitaller, porter and so forth. Orchards, piggeries, forge, tannery, mills all contributed to satisfying the needs of the community, producing materials for sale outside as well as for everyday domestic use. Leather from raw hides and skins produced belts, knife sheaths, shoes; calf and sheep skins were used for various grades of material, for writing accounts, official letters and documents, and for manuscripts for library and use in church. Probably the two Hailes chronicles were written on skins set aside for the purpose — anonymous contributions to the abbey's history. Sheep also provided sheepskins for blankets and warmly lined boots and wool for tunics, hoods and habits.[4] Tallies were used for the exchange of goods within the monastery. According to the Beaulieu account book (which may have been an exemplar) each department was expected to render a weekly account.

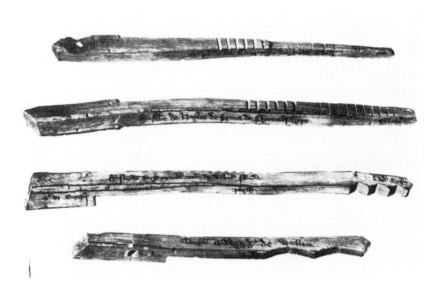

Tally sticks. The second from the top came from Pinnock

Hailes showed some relaxation of Cistercian regulations in its elaborate sculpture, architecture and fine tiles and its accumulation of property, but the visitation records of the abbots of Beaulieu reveal that, at least in the early decades, strenuous efforts were made to maintain Cistercian austerity and discipline. When Abbot Dennis visited Hailes in 1261, as his daughter house, he found the new community struggling and ordered that no more monks or lay-brothers should be added to the community until all debts had been cleared. More careful administration was required and the monks were to wash the church once a year, a necessity during the laying of tiles and the construction of tombs. So that the strictures should not be forgotten, the visitation report was to be read to the monks monthly. Nine years later Abbot John of Beaulieu found almsgiving at the Great Gate had ceased, presumably from lack of funds.[5] This reference to the Gate (whose site is not now known) is an indication that by the time work on the chevet was beginning the outer buildings of the monastery were in hand. Cistercian statutes required that 'stables of horses must be placed within the circuit of our abbeys, neither may any place of habitation be built outside the gate of the monastery unless for animals . . . if there be any, let them fall. Moreover let all the gates of the abbey be outside the bounds.' The gateway was the nearest point of contact with the outside world and, significantly, later visitation reports show stern measures to prevent disruption in that area. The statutes explained the prohibition as 'on account of the avoiding of souls'.[6] Abbot John also drew attention to the need for better care in the infirmary, possibly a temporary building at this time as, twenty years later, the abbey chronicle records the building of a new infirmary with adjoining buildings. Another stricture concerned the need to maintain the rule of silence and to avoid rushed chanting in the choir (an understandable fault, especially in an unheated building in winter). There is a remon-strance against flesh-eating and the keeping of dogs within the precincts; they were allowed in granges (home farms). Note was taken at the time of the need to keep an eye on young monks and their absence from services. The monks were warned that lights in the dormitory should be extinguished; many monastic fires were caused by candles falling on straw mattresses and Henry III's oak would have burnt well![7] The overall picture is of a community struggling to settle down.

Hailes derived much of its income throughout the three centuries of its history from the great flocks of sheep which grazed on the Cotswolds, as they still do in the vicinity of the abbey. Hailes was one of the English monasteries producing fine wool which earned a place in the famous 14th-century list of the Italian factor, Pegalotti.

Twenty sacks a year — at eighteen marks first quality, ten second, and seven marks third quality — were recorded. On the basis of an estimated 120 fleeces a sack this implies some four thousand sheep. (Beaulieu had flocks of between five and six thousand at this time.) Richard had given Hailes 120 acres of sheep pasture at Lower Swell, and his son, Edmund, later confirmed this gift. At the Dissolution there were six hundred sheep in the 'monks' close'.[8] Such flocks were not always popular with villages, especially during the 16th century, as the outcry against sheep farming in Bishop Latimer's sermons and the pamphlets of the time show. The copyholders of Longborough petitioned the Chancery Court against the Abbot of Hailes who, they asserted, had over nine hundred sheep on their village lands and was trying to drive them out by converting arable land to pasture. The last abbot of Hailes, in a letter written from Yorkshire to try to solve a boundary dispute between two new owners of monastery land at Farmcote and Coscombe (above Hailes), referred to 'divers shepherds in the area' who would know far more about the boundaries than he would. 'We kept the pasturing in our own hands', he wrote, and with precise recollection listed the familiar landmarks. He must have had a mental picture of the great flocks grazing above Hailes in the spring mornings when he was in his country mansion at Coscombe.

In 1256, there was a dispute with Bartholomew, Lord of Sudeley, about rights of common. A jury of twenty-four men, representing equally both parties, adjudicated and defined the areas 'in and out of common'. The area was a large one extending from Sudeley to Ford and including Greet and Pyseley. The list of names of the boundaries is most evocative of the rural setting: Gosehom, Sperewehomme, Sheepsbridge, Knight's Mead, Smitheshomme, Woderoweshomme.[9] Later the abbot had to pay on behalf of the abbey damages of 3s. $7^1/_2$d. when lambs from the abbey flock sought pasture in land belonging to Winchcombe parish church.

The accounts of Beaulieu, and those of the Cistercian monastery of Kingswood, help to bring alive the work involved with such flocks. In both cases outside shepherds were employed and every stage of the process, from the movement of flocks to new pastures to the sale of wool, is recorded: the purchase of tar for medicinal purposes, ewes for breeding (purchased in Lincolnshire), washing and shearing the sheep, collecting and grading the wood according to quality, and the sale of wool, fleeces or carcasses to outside buyers.

By the end of the 13th century, Hailes had acquired a considerable amount of land and income. Richard had given land at Swell and the abbey had a mill there.[10] By 1306, there were 250 acres at Swell and there had been a clash with the Abbey of Fécamp because the Abbot of Hailes would not allow his tenants there to attend Court Leet.

In 1270 Hailes acquired the fee-farm of Pinnock where there was another mill. An exchequer tally of the 13th century survives which records in its notches £16 6s 10d annual rent. It is inscribed: 'Abbé de Hayles de ferma de Pinnockschyre'.[11]

In 1291 two mills were recorded at Hailes itself, when the abbey contributed 106 shillings towards an appeal for a crusade launched by the Council of Lyons.[12]

Edmund's death in 1300 saw the end of the legitimate line of Richard, Earl of Cornwall, and the Earldom reverted to the Crown. It was a grievous loss for the abbey, for not only had Edmund been a generous and interested patron, but he had given the Holy Blood, underwritten the cost of the chevet and donated the gold and enamel cross with its fragment reputed to be from the True Cross. His gift of estates had helped the abbey's revenues. Abbot Hugh of Hailes was one of the executors of Edmund's will. His gifts had included Hemel Hempstead church, North Leigh (Oxfordshire), and probably the churches of St Breage and St Paul in Cornwall. He also gave the manor of Lechlade at a fee-farm of 100 marks.

Edmund's heir, Edward I, was present at his funeral at Hailes, staying overnight at Winchcombe Abbey. The Abbot of Tewkesbury was requested to attend the funeral.[13]

In 1325 the monks were struggling in debt and they petitioned the Bishop of Worcester in words which were an indirect tribute to their patrons of the foundation years: 'The Founders while they lived were wont to succour the monks generously in all their needs'.

It was indeed a misfortune for the monks that they were saddled with a very large building, with no patrons to help in the century of economic and social upheaval that was upon them. Edward I was otherwise occupied, and there is more evidence of demands than of gifts from him! His own foundation of Vale Royal found this to their cost. Their plea to Edward III provides an illustration of what befell a monastery when funds dried up. They wrote: 'We have a very large church begun by the king of England at our first foundation but by no means finished . . . he built it with stone walls but the crypt remains to be built with the roof and glass and other ornaments of the church.' They went on to say that other parts of the monastery needed rebuilding in the same style to match the church.

5. HAILES PARISH CHURCH

The little parish church was about a century old when it came into the possession of the abbey.[1] Cistercian statutes forbade monasteries of its Order to become rectors of churches and thereby secure income from that source. Hailes, however, was a late foundation with an influential patron, and the church remained under its special jurisdiction until the dissolution of the monastery when it reverted once more to parish use. It was probably used by the monks as a 'chapel at the gate' for visitors to the monastery.

The link with Richard of Cornwall and his family can be seen in the large painted coats of arms which decorate the south chancel wall in an elaborate grid. The arms of his Earldom of Cornwall, and of the Kingdom of the Romans, are there with those associated with Sanchia of Provence, his second wife, and Beatrix von Falkenburg, his widow.[2] On the north wall are the arms of Edward I's first wife, Eleanor of Castille, with further German eagles. Two panels of smaller arms include those of England, Scotland,[3] the Honour of St Valery,[4] and de Clare,[5] as well as those of many families whose names loomed large in the baronial wars.

Visitors to the church today are most likely to be interested in the fascinating wall paintings, all of which were created during the abbey's possession of the church. A beautiful, early 14th-century painting of St Catherine of Alexandria, book in hand, with the Emperor Maximin (or Maxentius), her persecutor, now scarcely visible under her feet, stands in a half-blocked window splay in the north chancel wall. Facing her is St Margaret, piercing a very jaunty, large-clawed dragon with the long shaft of a cross. Each figure is accompanied by a small, black-habited figure, possibly that of a donor. Both saints have an elegant, gracefully curved posture and cascading folds of garments.

Two censing angels are ranged on either side of the east window,[6] their feet gently curved along the border. Under the wall plate is the remains of a frieze which possibly illustrated the apostles and scenes from the life of Christ or the Virgin.[7] The brushwork of these figures, still discernible, is of high quality.

For many people, however, it is the animals that are most fascinating.

St Catherine. 14th-century in the splay of the north chancel window, Hailes parish Church

14th-century paintings of strange creatures in the spandrels of the chancel windows in Hailes parish church

Tiles from east end of the abbey church, c. 1270

A short-eared owl keeps watch on a twig at the corner of the west-most arch of the sedilia. The beak of a bird faces him from the other side of the arch. In the spandrels of the windows above are pairs of strange creatures facing each other in combat. Among their ranks is an elephant with gleaming eye and winged back; a satyr; a white unicorn with long tapering horn; several wyverns and a basilisk. On the north wall a goat and hare are engaged in mock battle with sword and buckler. These animals must have derived from medieval bestiaries or border scenes in contemporary books of hours or psalters.[8] Medieval preachers would have found there ample illustration for their sermons. Those who recognised creatures from allegories and fables could provide their own morals.

In the nave, on the south wall, is a splendid coursing scene where a petrified hare crouches under a tree (drawn with the delicacy of a Japanese painting) while three hunting dogs, eyes alight with anticipation, ears pricked and tails pointing, leap forward. Behind, horn to mouth and shield over his arm, is the much mutilated figure of a huntsman.[9] The scene is full of vitality, one can almost smell the rich brown earth beneath their feet. The artist was clearly a craftsman of sensitivity and quality. The significance of the painting is now lost; it could represent a country scene of the kind that appears in psalters of the time, or recall some person or incident in the history of the abbey. Whatever its purpose the artist has left a scene worth preserving. When the setting sun lights the wall the scene becomes alive with an almost magical quality.

The activity in the church in the early decades of the 14th century soon gave way to a period of gloom and retrenchment in the abbey itself. It was well into the 15th century before the fabric of either received much further embellishment.

The remaining wall paintings in the nave of the parish church are scarcely discernible. There is a small naked figure just west of the blocked north door, and this may represent a soul from a lost Doom painting. Between the blocked door and the 17th-century pulpit is a huge St Christopher with the Christ Child on his shoulder. This 15th-century figure takes almost the full height of the wall. At his feet incisions in the wall gave a faint indication of ships and waves. The patron saint of travellers faces the south door, apparently the only entrance in monastic times.

6. THE MIDDLE YEARS

This famous realm of England which used to rejoice in the beauty of peace is now afflicted and rent and divided. We intend therefore, with the advice and consent of our Suffragans, to invoke the aid of Heaven against the disturbers of the peace and grant heavenly rewards to those who defend it.
Archbishop Winchelsea: letter to the Bishop of Worcester, 1317.

The upheavals of the 14th century afflicted monasteries everywhere. Natural disasters, abnormally bad weather, failing harvests and crops, with cattle disease, were followed by famine and soaring prices. Plague and sickness, culminating in the Black Death of 1348-9 (and the renewed outbreaks of 1361, 1368, 1369, 1375, 1390 and 1391), led to a shortage of labour of every kind and demands for higher wages. This was at a time when a surplus of land reduced its value and prices of agricultural goods fell. The Hailes chronicle mirrors the times:

1301   On the Feast of the Assumption of the Blessed Virgin there was thunder and terrible lightning and rain such as we have not known in our time. The storm lasted throughout the whole night.

1319-20   A great famine arose throughout the whole of England because everything failed in England and France and a quarter of corn was sold for 40 shillings.

1321   A great mortality took place among men such as had never before been seen.

1337   On the Vigil of Corpus Christi about the hour of Vespers, a sudden flood of water arose in the monastery of Hailes which brought about serious damage, loss and distress.

1348   There came so great a plague in the land that of every three men, scarce one remained. At the same time a quarter of corn was sold for twelve pence, a quarter of winter barley for nine pence, a measure of salt for eight pence, a draught animal for six pence, one good ox for forty pence, a good horse for six shillings, a good cow for two shillings and eight pence. And for all these prices a purchaser could scarce be found.

The last entry gives a picture of the agricultural problems of the monks. They must have felt, as they struggled, that even the weather was against them. It is not surprising that they sought what help they could and made sure of what they had. In this connection there arose the affair of Pyseley Warren, near the junction of the Salt Way and the path to Winchcombe. The monks of Hailes had, by royal grant, the right of warren there, which meant no one without licence could

Seal of Hailes Abbey 1425
GRO GBR JI/1089

hunt for game, hare, partridge or rabbits.[1] Winchcombe Abbey held tithes for part of a meadow at Pyseley and there occurred a case of trespass by the Abbot of Winchcombe's dogs in the warren. It is conceivable that the coursing scene in the parish church at Hailes had some connection with this affair. It was settled by a meeting between Walter, Abbot of Winchcombe, and Hugh, Abbot of Hailes, in 1301, when they met at Greet, in St Laurence's church. The two monasteries had several disputes about tithes in the area near the river Isborne, on the borderland between the two monasteries.

There was trouble, too, further away from home. Edmund had given Hailes the fee-farm of his manor of Lechlade for 100 marks a year. But his successor, Edward I, possibly in view of the economic situation, demanded a rent of £100 instead, so that Lechlade became a liability rather than a source of income. Even more of a problem to the monks was the collection of rents from their distant Cornish churches. In 1327 the King 'guaranteed protection and safe conduct for two years to Richard Gloucester and John Cherney (Cerney?), monks of Hailes, sent by their abbot who is parson of the churches of St Paul and St Breage and St Corontus to take charge of these churches and collect the fruits (income) and obventions and profits to his use'. It must have been a daunting journey in those troubled times![2] In 1337 the abbey requested further help from the King against 'persons who threatened and assaulted the abbey's men in Cornwall and their servants and carried away their goods'. By the end of the century the abbey had decided to lease out the churches at rent. Even then their problems were not over: in 1395 some of their Cornish tenants were outlawed for non-payment of dues; nevertheless, the abbey still held the churches at the usual income of £88 annually when the monastery was dissolved.

It is understandable, therefore, that the monks petitioned the Bishop of Worcester for help because their 'rents and issues of distant places and remote dioceses yield little or nothing when their obligations are discharged'. In an attempt to stabilise their economic position the monks asked to be allowed to appropriate[3] Longborough church and, later, Toddington with its chapel at Stanley Pontlarge. The provisions made for the vicars of such churches are interesting. At Longborough, for example, the vicar's stipend was to be not less than ten pounds a year, and he was to be granted the rectory house with adjoining land, dovecote (an important source of food), tithes in hay, calves, pigs, geese, burial fees and other customary offerings. In return, the vicar was to maintain lights in the chancel, sufficient books, vestments and ornaments necessary for divine service. The abbot and convent of Hailes, on their part, were to be responsible for the repair of the chancel and roof. Similar provisions were made later in the century for Toddington church, where the vicar had to provide processional candles, incense and communion needs for Easter, while the abbot paid ten marks and gave three pounds of wax for candles for processions and services, and all the lights for the Feast of Purification. The monks' petition lists the many problems which confronted them in the way of insufficient revenue:

Whereas the founders when they lived were wont to succour the monks generously in their need, the advowson of the abbey devolved on the King who burdens them with certain perpetual residents.

The latter were corrodians[4] such as 'Sampson the Venour' (huntsman), Adam and William de Brokholes, who were described as having been long in royal service, and in need of the necessities of life in the shape of food and clothing, 'according to the requirements of their estate'. Sampson's presence is noteworthy in view of the possible connection with the coursing scene in the parish church. Cistercian statutes had been framed to avoid contact with the world, hence they provided that the great gate should be removed from the life of the community. The presence of royal pensioners, with time and capacity for gossip, must have been a considerable distraction to the monks although it is possible that some of them, like Sampson, were able to offer helpful advice in the practice of their skills. Later requests from the royal courts were in the form of money grants from estates held by the monastery, such as the 100 shillings from the Manor of Pinnock for the King's confessor, 'broken by age', living in Beverley (1352), and a similar request in 1394 for a Thomas Shepey.

Another source of grievance of the monks, referred to in their petition, was the heavy demand for hospitality expected of them as monks:

the monastery is on a high road and the arrival of rich men and lords and poor, together with imposts and collections which get greater day by day cause them to submit lest worse befall.

Finally, the monks referred to the weather and general state of unrest:

the leanness of recent years and the cattle plague and the extortions of enemies have caused a burden of debt they know not how to meet in their distress without help from outside.

Royal exactions went beyond the retired royal pensioners as the monks indicate. In 1276, Edward I had asked for the 'courtesy' — levies of corn, cattle, horses, wagons for transport and supply for the royal army in Scotland.[5] They paid £14 13s 4d as an 'Aid' to Edward.[6] In 1311 there was another 'Aid' in the shape of a loan with victuals (various amounts of wheat, malt, beans, peas, oats, beef and sheep) for Scotland. In 1338, the King was asking 'without delay' for a strong horse to carry Chancery rolls. In 1340, Edward III levied his Inquisition of Ninths, demanding every ninth sheaf, fleece and lamb for the maintenance and safeguard of the realm. The abbot, in addition, was burdened with the task of acting as one of the assessors in the district.

Dues were demanded by the Church. In 1299 the abbot was given absolution for having paid a subsidy to royal tax gatherers against a papal prohibition. He was pardoned, with the penance of feeding forty poor persons, on the grounds that he had feared what might befall him if he did not pay! In 1291 the abbey had to contribute to taxation granted by Pope Nicholas IV upon temporal possessions of religious houses in England. The monks must have greeted every messenger with apprehension as the demands flowed inexorably in.

The request for a horse to carry state records brings to mind a letter written by the chaplain of Harwell (copy in the abbey museum) with a tactfully couched demand for the purchase of a horse for his own use:

As I should like to hear good news of your health and safety I am writing to you to send me by the bearer news of yourself and my friends in the neighbourhood and since, having lost some of my horses, I am hardly able to go about and there is at present a fair at Winchcombe near you where I have often heard many horses are to be found. I beg you to look about you and get some of your people to give their advice and help the bearer so that I may be provided with a suitable horse there costing not more than four or five marks.[7]

Fortunately for the monks, small bequests did come in from private individuals. Sir Robert Russell had given them Knight's Meadow (later called Monks' Meadow) near Greet mill on the Isborne, in line with Ireley farm. In 1312-13, John Sage granted land in Brockhampton. In 1342, John Benn gave eighty-two acres of land and fourteen acres of meadow in Newington, Toddington, Farmcote and Sudeley. The Prince of Wales asked Edward III to grant the abbey licence to acquire lands and rents to the value of twenty pounds a year.

Sometimes Hailes was asked to provide contributions for its own Order, as in 1400 when the English Cistercians had to contribute to the support of their scholars at Oxford. Hailes paid £4 6s. 8d.[8]

Another expense arose when members of the community were presented for ordination. Their names, as they appear in the episcopal registers, indicate the local origin of many of the monks: 1309, John of Pershore and John of Barton were priested at

Cirencester; 1322, Richard of Evesham and Robert of Didbrook were made sub-deacons; 1313, John Flaxley, Thomas Harwell priests; 1343, Richard Dumbleton a priest and Walter Sedgeberrow deacon; and, in 1343, John Cheltenham and Walter Prestbury deacons. Travel expenses for these candidates must have been heavy as they followed the bishop around the diocese.

Among the monks of Hailes in the 14th century was one of the six sons of Lord Harley, all of whom were placed in monasteries. The Worcester records include a letter from John, the eldest, to Roger, the youngest, encouraging him to persevere in the religious life 'now the Prince of Darkness has been conquered you may for the future be a child of light and the Good Shepherd has placed on His shoulders the wandering sheep and brought it back to the fold'.

Cistercian monasteries relied on the produce of their lands for a steady income, exploiting their fields by the labour of lay-brothers (*conversi*) who worked on the granges (home farms) set up in open country some miles from the monastery. They would return to the abbey on Sundays and feast days except at times of intensive labour, such as harvest. These granges were worked as individual farms producing crops of wheat, barley, oats, rye, vetch, peas, beans, or keeping pigs, cattle and sheep as well as breeding them: they also served as collecting centres for produce which was delivered for sale or use to the abbey.

Considerable light is thrown on the nature of a grange by events recorded at the Hailes grange at Wormington, a few miles away — violence of a kind all too common in contemporary records. In 1318 the abbot complained that his bridge over the river Lindbrook had been broken down, the road obstructed by trenches dug across it, his cattle impounded, his corn trampled down, his men assaulted so that he could find no one willing to work for him. There was more trouble on the same grange in 1345 when Sir William Dastyn and others broke into the abbot's close and houses at Wormington and drove off horses, oxen, sheep and swine worth 100 marks.

Marauding bands troubled the abbeys at Winchcombe and Hailes. In 1366 the Pope commissioned the abbots of Hailes, Cirencester, Evesham and Winchcombe to act as judges for five years against those who detained property and to help secure restitution.

Much of the unrest in the second half of the 14th century was a consequence of the Black Death of 1348-9 and its subsequent outbreaks. Gloucestershire and the area about the Severn suffered badly. At Bristol it was recorded that 'the living could scarce bury the dead'. Gloucester, in a vain attempt to escape, refused all contact with the stricken city. Nineteen out of thirty canons at Llanthony Priory, Gloucester, died and that monastery lost nearly all its rents and services by the death of tenants. Winchcombe Abbey fell into serious debt as the Bishop of Worcester noted when he referred to their 'barren lands reduced rents and services reduced by half because of the death of tenants and servants from past pestilence'. He also marked buildings ruined by frightful gales. At Cirencester the Black Prince had endowed a chantry 'bearing in mind the poverty of the canons there after the late mortality of men happening in England causing loss of income so great that the Canons could not maintain hospitality or even keep up their own numbers, let alone repair the formerly sumptuously built parts of their monastery now collapsed in ruins'.

The See of Worcester was, significantly, vacant when in 1350 Edward III appealed 'for prayers and fasting and repentance of sins throughout the country so God in his pity may drive away the plague and sickness and grant peace and tranquility and salvation both to body and soul . . . for we hope, by God's grace, that if the people cast out from their hearts spiritual wickedness as well as the scourge of the air, this as well as other tempests may depart from them . . . We dread the fear of the remnants of the people so wretched who have survived'. Hailes could not have escaped the impact of the plague although no details of numbers who perished survive. In 1364, a Sunday, the chronicle records:

some satellites of Satan broke into the vestry of Hailes by force and stole sacred vessels — some patens, 11 chalices worth 40s (at least three of them and that of the high altar 100s) besides two chasubles worth 12 silver pounds and two thuribles worth £22.

We do not know whether the huge beam holes to take great bars right across the threshold of the church processional door into the cloister, the vestry and the undercroft, were made as a result of this incident. The bars should have been proof against any force.

At Hailes, as elsewhere, the Black Death by its sudden onset and severity precipitated changes already taking place in society. Loss of workers and low prices led to the break up of many estates and the leasing of churches. These changes coincided with the disappearance of lay-brothers and the employment of a large number of outside workers (seventy servants of the monastery are recorded at the Dissolution). The lay-brothers' range in the west cloister became the abbot's house and, in the next century, was to be considerably altered and embellished.[9] There is no certain evidence that Hailes had the customary lane adjoining the west cloister walk to separate lay-brothers from the choir monks, but the cloister was rebuilt in the 15th century. The lay brothers' entrance into the church and the site of the night stairs to their dormitory survive.

In these troubled times it is not surprising that there are references to recalcitrant monks. In 1364 a Hailes monk, John Andover, who was in priest's orders and had left the monastery, went to Avignon to petition the Pope to help him to return. The Pope advised that he should be treated leniently. In 1403 another Hailes monk was found wandering around in secular clothes at Oxford. When the monastery petitioned the Bishop to be allowed to appropriate Toddington church (Sir John Tracy had given them the advowson in 1363) they gave as their reason the lack of adequate clothing and food for the monks.

Abbot Herman from Beaulieu, who visited Hailes in 1394, requested more devout and solemn chanting in the choir and the clearance of weeds from the cloisters. Four years later there was comment about absentees from divine service and the need for better care for the sick as well as for silence in the cloisters. Observation on the lack of adequate clothing for the monks confirms the truth of their petition for Toddington. The Visitors recommended that money from the abbey's churches in Rodborough (Wiltshire) and North Leigh (Oxfordshire) should be set aside for the purpose.

In 1442, there was a further reference to absence from the choir and to the low standard of singing, as well as to the old problem of contact with lay people at the gatehouse and the consequent need to replace the gatekeeper.

Loss of revenue and manpower are the reason for grants to the monastery to permit their monks to serve churches in the vicinity which belonged to the abbey. In 1413, Pope John XXIII accepted their petition to use one of their monks as vicar at Didbrook 'because through various sinister events their income has become so much diminished that it is insufficient for the sustenance of their twenty-two monks and their servants nor for hospitality and other burdens'. Another monk had been given permission to serve at Pinnock church. This had always been a poor living; as early as 1313 there were complaints that the priest in charge had allowed many defects in the chancel, in books, ornaments and in the manse, which had been there in the time of his predecessor. John Stanlake, a Hailes monk, was now allowed 'if found fit in Latin' to serve Pinnock church which 'had wont to be served by a secular clerk'. The value of the church in income was minute, not exceeding 3½ marks, so it is not surprising that 'in consequence of the rarity of priests in these parts and on account of the smallness of the stipend no secular priest could be found willing to be instituted'. Another Hailes monk was given permission to serve at Longborough. All three churches were still being served by monks of Hailes at the Dissolution. Earlier in the century a monk of Hailes had written to the Prior of Benedictine Worcester to express his concern about their church at Stratton-on-the-Fosse. The monastery had apparently delayed in appointing a new vicar and the monk piously expressed his fears that the parishioners were in danger of dying without baptism or confession. The Prior replied that, because two patrons were involved, time was needed before a decision was made and he added, tartly, that a Benedictine prior would act with the same deliberation as a Cistercian! No doubt Hailes had some bruised feelings about visitations from priors of Worcester to churches in their care.[10]

Hailes had by now acquired a string of rentals for shops and tenements in Gloucester and this led to a dispute with the Hospital of St Bartholomew there, founded by King Henry III. An agreement was reached, on 20 September 1426, between Stephen, Prior of the hospital, and William, Abbott of Hailes and their convents, concerning the rents for tenements in South Street, near All Saints Church, which both sides claimed. Hailes proved that by charter they held the tenements by fealty and at a rent of 6s. 8d. and they agreed that they owned that rent and service, while the Prior and brothers of the hospital confirmed that they were not entitled to more than that. Appended to the document (now in the Record Office) is a splendid Hailes seal showing a Virgin and Child enthroned against an elaborate ground reminiscent of a rose window.

In 1395 a monk of Hailes, John of Gloucester, was nominated by the English Cistercian Chapter to be abbot of Beaulieu, but there was a disputed election and considerable friction, involving armed men. Another Hailes monk, William of Elmley, had apparently been wrongly imprisoned for about a year by the abbey, or so his friends claimed. A papal mandate ordered the abbot of Winchcombe and an official of the bishop to see he was restored to full rights and privileges by Hailes.

It was another half century before the scene became less troubled. As late as 1442 visiting abbots insisted that an abbot of Hailes should render annual accounts, and appointed two bursars from among the monks to supervise all money received and expended. Internal and external repairs to the abbey were ordered and the general state of discipline was criticised. In French Cistercian archives[11] there survives a letter written by Abbot John Crombeck of Hailes asking for exemption for a time from payment of subsidies due 'because of the pitiable administration' of his predecessor. The struggle to maintain a large monastic complex with a small number of monks in a changing society was a challenge for any abbot. The Papal indulgences given by 15th-century popes to pilgrims (see Chapter 3) repeatedly refer to the real needs of the abbey: ruined buildings, insufficient funds for twenty-two monks, food and hospitality. One of the more forceful abbots, William, went in person to Rome to plead the abbey's needs, leaving the prior, John Alster, in charge with two monks as advisors. All valuables were locked away in the treasury and the convent seal kept in safe custody so that no official business could be undertaken secretly without the community being involved. In 1480, an abbot of Hailes was one of the commissioners sent to inspect Welsh Cistercian houses with a view to reform.

Towards the end of the 15th century the tide began to turn and for the last half century of its existence Hailes experienced a period of recovery and near-prosperity.

7. RECOVERY

The material fortunes of the abbey improved considerably under the last six abbots. The 'Little Treatise on Divers Miracles'(1519) suggests that pilgrims were being more actively encouraged and the existence of the Confraternity of Hailes may have brought new patrons to the abbey. There is evidence for increased prosperity in the encaustic tiles commemorating, in particular, two of the abbots, Thomas Stratford and Anthony Melton. Sixteen-tile sets include their initials with an abbot's crozier and mitre and puns on their names: Staff and Ford, Mel and Tun (a barrel), with decorative motifs of birds (ducks to go with the ford?), stylized flowers and little creatures to balance the elaborate interlace which holds the patterns together. Such Tudor conceits would have horrified early Cistercians! The royal founder of Hailes was not forgotten: a particularly fine representation of his arms, both as Earl of Cornwall and as King of Germany, is set off in a counter-change pattern. *Fleurs-de-lys* (in various forms), the arms of England, Despenser and Beauchamp appear in other designs. There is a Tudor portcullis (for Beaufort) and a pomegranate for Catherine of Aragon, with charming variations on the Tudor rose. These tiles were until recently preserved at Southam de la Bere but are now on display, some in the abbey museum and some in the British Museum. Such personal advertisement as is shown in the Stafford and Melton tiles is characteristic of the more worldly atmosphere of the times. The abbey cloisters, rebuilt in the late 15th century, belong to a similar exuberant spirit. Remains of the fan vaulting can be seen near the processional door into the cloisters and over the lavatory in the south cloister; and the angel corbels bearing shields[1] survive on part of the north cloister walk, adjoining the church. The three inner cloister arches in the west cloister were protected by the extension of the abbot's house over that cloister walk. Heraldic bosses found in that area (now on display in the museum) indicate that work was continuing in this part almost until the Dissolution. Among the arms represented were those of Sir John Huddleston and his wife, Joan. He had been Constable of Sudeley Castle and of Gloucester Castle, as well as sheriff twice and had attended the funeral of Henry VII. Sir John and his wife were generous patrons of the abbey as their wills illustrate. Sir John made the abbot of Hailes his executor, leaving him ten pounds for his pains. He requested:

My body to be buried within the monastery of Hailes before Our Lady of Pity . . . there should be laid over me a stone of marble with a picture of myself therein and writing thereupon to make mention of my departing.

He left money for masses for his soul and that of his wife to be said daily for eight years and then made two practical contributions:

£20 for amending the way that goeth forth from the said monastery towards Pyseley Hill and for the way that goeth from the said monastery towards Winchcombe.[2]

Sir John, who died in 1511 or 1512, must have walked those paths many times. His charity would have been welcomed by weary pilgrims at the end of long journeys. Lady Huddleston survived until 1518 or 1519, and was probably living at Hailes as a corrodian at the time. Her will was made 'in my chamber at Hailes' in the presence of 'my ghostly Father, the prior', to whom she bequeathed two carpets, two green feather cushions and a pillow. Like her husband, she asked for burial in the abbey 'afore the image of Our Lady of Pity and within the chapel of St Nicholas where my tomb is ready made'.

She left to the altar of this chapel 'an altar cloth of purple damask with Our Lady and St George and St Martin embroidered therein'.[3]

The other items mentioned in her will seem to have come from her apartment within the abbey:

two curtains of sarcenet fringed at the ends, an altar cloth of purple damask with garlands embroidered thereon. A chalice with paten, a corporas case of cloth of gold with pearls, a Mass Book and a crucifix now upon the altar within my chamber, two linen cloths two towels for the altar and a pax of silver with two cruets of silver.

Two down cushions and two black velvet gowns, one lined with fur, were left to the convent 'to make ornaments at the cost of the convent at their pleasure'. To the vestry at Hailes she left a 'chest bounden with iron and three locks'. It may have been the one used later to send the relic of the Holy Blood to London to be examined and then destroyed. After the customary provision for masses, Lady Huddleston made an interesting proviso: 'If I die before all the aisles of the abbey church at Hailes are fully finished, leaded and embattled, it should be finished by my executors at my cost without delay'. Here is evidence that building alterations were in progress at Hailes at this time. There is a similar reference to the church at Winchcombe: 'If I die before the chapel of Our Lady of Winchcombe be finished it shall be at my proper cost without delay'. The embattlementing mentioned at Hailes recalls that of Winchcombe parish church, and the remains of a waterspout in the form of a Tudor matron found in the west cloister at Hailes (now in the museum), resembles the gargoyles at Winchcombe. There was plenty to keep masons busy in the district. Lady Huddleston's will was given into the safe-keeping of the Abbot of Hailes 'in a little casket locked with the lock hole sealed with my seal'.

Another benefactor at this time was John Shoo, parson of Dowdeswell, who in his will directed:

I give my body for burial in the monastery of the Holy Blood at Hailes . . . I give a vestment of black, unhallowed, a gift to the monastery. To be provided to Master Selener of Hailes, a Mass Book, presented, my knife that I ride with, also 'Sermones discipli'.

There was a William Shoo among the Hailes monks at the Dissolution.

In Wells Cathedral library two illuminated manuscripts, a Psalter and a Commentary on St John Chrysostom, are associated with Hailes. The frontispiece of the Psalter, showing Psalm 1, is inscribed *Liber Monasterii de Hayles*. It shows King David playing a harp before a vested abbot, both kneeling, against a background scene of a distant city. God, in the act of blessing, is revealed in the sky above. The border is decorated with poppies, wild strawberries, daisies, clover leaves and heartsease. The arms of Christopher Urswyck, formerly great almoner to King Henry VII, appear in both manuscripts. These are confirmed by an inscription in the Psalter stating that the work was done for Sir Christopher, as the last wish of Sir John Huddleston in perpetual memory of his wife and himself, by Peter Meghen, a German scribe then resident in Brussels.

Abbot William Whytchurch, whose initials may be those on the Buckland Cope, is credited with the rebuilding of Didbrook church as well as the rebuilding programme at Hailes. Bishop Carpenter consecrated the church at Didbrook on 18 June 1472, after an earlier inquisition about the pollution of the church by bloodshed.[4] The abbot's name appears in a damaged and abbreviated Latin inscription in the church window which originally read 'Pray for the soul of

Psalm 1 in the Hailes Psalter, written by Peter Meghen in 1514, now in Wells Cathedral Library. The arms are those of Christopher Urswyck. Dean and Chapter of Wells

William Whytchurch who founded this church with the chancel'. It is possible that the glass, like that of the east window in the parish church of Hailes, came originally from the abbey, perhaps from the abbot's house which was embellished at this time.⁵ However, Didbrook belonged to the abbey which was responsible for its upkeep. Rebuilding at Didbrook with battlementing was clearly in progress at the time.

The other west cloister armorial bosses at Hailes are linked to Henry Percy, Earl of Northumberland (d. 1527) whose household book shows that he contributed money annually for lights for the Holy Blood of Hailes, and to Sir John Compton who succeeded Huddleston at Sudeley. Compton left money to Hailes for masses for the King and Queen and for his family, but Winchcombe Abbey got his wedding gown of tinsel to make vestments! The last surviving boss bears the arms of Evesham Abbey but that link remains obscure.

Pilgrims who were visiting the shrine in considerable numbers must have been interested to see the work going on there, and were doubtless told of benefactions of patrons to encourage their own contributions. The abbey church stood with its roof and aisles nearly restored and improved, the abbot's house had been improved and the new cloisters would attract attention.

All this must have led the convent to feel, as the commissioners were to note in 1539, that Hailes might go on for ever. But the world outside was changing and changing very fast.

8. THE LAST DAYS OF HAILES

We have taken the surrender of the late monastery of Hailes where we found the Father and his brothers very honest and conformable persons and the House very clearly out of debt. *The King's Commissioners to Thomas Cromwell, 4 January, 1540.*

Hailes Abbey was formally dissolved on Christmas Eve, 1539, a few weeks after Winchcombe Abbey. From surviving correspondence it is clear that Stephen Sagar,[1] the last abbot, was, at least outwardly, on good terms with Thomas Cromwell. He had complied with his request in 1531 for one of Cromwell's nominees to occupy one of the abbey farms at Longborough.

At Hailes, as elsewhere, the Injunctions, which ostensibly set out to help the monasteries reform themselves, made life difficult for the community. The monks were required to listen to a daily commentary on the New Testament in English. Abbot Sagar explained his problem to Cromwell:

I have none of my brethren so perfectly learned that I may put my trust in him to read the scriptures to my brethren according to the injunctions unless I have some of my scholars from Oxford which I am loath to do.

Eventually a scholar of Divinity, called Curtis, was secured from Magdalen College, Oxford, and Abbot Sagar wrote: 'He did read before me and my brethren two or three lessons very substantially'.

Curtis was no supporter of advanced reforming ideas; indeed he had not yet taken the oath of loyalty to the King's succession and hastened to do so. A reforming cleric sent to Winchcombe Abbey and active in the district was soon complaining bitterly about Curtis to Cromwell:

The abbot of Hailes, a valiant soldier under Anti-Christ's banner resists much, fighting with all his might to keep Christ in his sepulchre. He hired a great Goliath, a subtle Duns Man,[2] a great clerk so he saith, bachelor in Divinity to catch me in my sermons.

It is difficult to assess where Abbot Sagar stood with regard to the new learning and the ideas of the reformers. His attitude was always diplomatic and conciliatory. He wrote to Cromwell about the required reading of commentaries from the scriptures: 'I am glad to see the light. I should never have come to that light if I had not the liberty to read the scriptures in English'.

Among the letters of Brother Joseph, a monk of Evesham Abbey who showed considerable enthusiasm for the new learning and classical revival, were some to a monk of Hailes whom he had met studying at Oxford, evidence that new ideas were current among some of the monks.[3]

The abbot was troubled by another Injunction, the order not to increase the number of the monks. Sagar wrote to Cromwell, who had been in the district recently: 'At your last being here you bade me show you what I needed. I beg dispensation for the following five articles enclosed'.

He accompanied this request for the relaxation of restrictions with the customary gift, in this case 'a poor token of good will . . . a strange piece of gold'. The abbot put his case for increasing the number of monks: 'The number of my brethren is sore decayed, two I have buried, three are at Oxford at Divinity. I beg that I may take in more to help in the choir.'

There follows an explanation, that, contrary to Cistercian statutes, Hailes monks were serving in churches appropriated to the abbey: 'The churches and chapels where my brethren have served in accordance to old grants' Sagar then ventures an inspired suggestion:

If I might be so bold. I would suggest you would moderate your injunctions upon my poor arbitrament and then if anything were amiss it would be upon my jeopardy — if I find it necessary to release some of them. You can withdraw the liberty at any time.

There is no evidence that Cromwell took the hint but relations continued pleasant.

In 1537, Abbot Sagar was made a royal chaplain, much to the discomfiture of Bishop Latimer who wrote to Cromwell: 'As for my Lord of Hailes, I fear (he) will be too Cockett now with his great authority and promotion'. In another letter the same bishop refers to 'the Bluddy Abbot', clearly a reference to the Holy Blood.

The troublesome Injunctions stated that relics were no longer to be exhibited for the increase of lucre 'and that money donated by pilgrims should be given instead to the poor'.

The famous shrine at Hailes now became the subject of enquiry.

Abbot Sagar hurried to clear this obstacle, writing to Cromwell: 'Your Honour knows that within the monastery of Hailes is a Blood which has been reputed for a miracle for great season'. He then goes on to explain that he is anxious to put aside anything which seems to favour superstition, but does not wish to appear to be doing anything on his own authority. He asked for a commission to investigate the matter, but at the same time vigorously refuted the story that the Blood was a fake renewed weekly by the monks with drake's blood. He wrote: 'There is a monk nearly eighty years old who has kept it almost forty years who will confirm this'.

Clearly Hailes was still a healthy place! It is interesting to speculate whether this venerable guardian of the shrine was the writer of 'Divers Miracles'. He, the abbot was certain, would confirm the abbot's sure knowledge that the relic was in the state in which it had come to the monastery and that it had not been tampered with since.

The appearance of the Blood can to some extent be envisaged from the ensuing correspondence. Cromwell sent commissioners, including the very critical Latimer, to examine the relic and they reported:

We have been bolting[4] and sifting the Blood of Hailes all the fore noon. It was wondrously and craftily enclosed and stopped up for the taking care. It cleaves fast to the bottom of the little glass it is in and verily it seemeth to be an unctuous gum, a compound of many things. It has certain unctuous moistness and though it seemeth somewhat like blood in the glass, yet when any parcel of the same is taken out it turneth to yellowness and is cleaving like gum.[5]

This letter conjures up a fascinating picture of Latimer and his companions poring over the relic to the consternation of the aged guardian of the shrine.

Even after all this analysis the commissioners were uncertain how to proceed. They wrote to Cromwell, 'We perceive not by your commission whether we shall send it up or leave it here'. They had 'enclosed it in red wax and consigned it with our seals and have locked it in a coffer with two locks[6] remaining by deed indented with the said abbot of Hailes, the other with . . . Richard Tracy'. Tracy was another commissioner and member of a local family who had given Toddington church to the abbey in the 14th century.

Two further pieces of information add to our knowledge of the famous relic before it disappears for ever. Abbot Sagar wrote to

Cromwell: 'Touching the value of the silver and gold that is therein I think it is not worth 20s. scant 30s. by estimation'.

This must have been the 'garnishing' that bound the bottle on every side. The certificate sent to Cromwell in October 1538 referred to the 'supposed relic' which had been 'tried according to our powers, wits and discretions by all means and by force of view and other trials'. The sermon given by the Bishop of Rochester at St Paul's Cross when the relic was finally destroyed described it as 'no blood but honey clarified and coloured with saffron as had been proved before the King and His Council'.

The abbot now worried whether the surviving shell of the shrine could be a source of trouble. Another letter to Cromwell sought permission 'to put down the case where that feigned relic, called the Blood was in . . . It doth stand as yet in the place still as it was in manner and fashion of a shrine'. He requested Cromwell to give licence 'that I may put it down every stick and stone that no manner or token of remembrance of that forged relic shall remain during the time it shall please Our Sovereign Lord the King's Majesty and your good Lordship that this poor House shall stand'.

Three years after the monastery had been dissolved, royal agents were inquiring into the disappearance of small items from the partly demolished site after the royal agents and landowners had taken their pick. A certain Richard Reeves, servant to Richard Andrews of Hailes, was given 'two painted boards from the altar where the Blood stood'. Anthony Griffiths of Didbrook had 'many hooks of iron wherewith the stories were hanged'. These boards hanging near the shrine presumably told the story of how the Blood was obtained and how it came to the abbey, as given in the abbey chronicle and the 'Little Treatise'. They may also have recorded some of the miracles wrought there. A visitor to Hailes in 1518 described how he saw and read the history of the bringing of the Blood which was 'written on a table just by the entering into that chapel where the relic was kept'.

Despite his apparently cordial contacts with Thomas Cromwell and his royal chaplaincy, Abbot Sagar was not able to save the monastery. He appears to have paved the way for final surrender on the best possible terms during a visit to London. Rumours spread by his enemies suggest that he was making sure that the King did not get full value from the abbey, but the royal agents wrote approvingly when they took surrender of Hailes Abbey on Christmas Eve 1539:

We have taken surrender of the late monastery of Hailes where we found the Father and his brothers very honest and conformable persons and the House clearly out of debt. Over that, the Father had his House and Grounds so well furnished with jewels, plate and stuff, corn, cattle and the woods well served as though he had looked for no alteration to his House. His arable land was in like manner husbanded, no small number of acres were ready sown with wheat and the tilth reasonably ordered for barley.

To the end the abbot acted with his usual discretion. The royal agents wrote: 'He did surrender his house with such discreet and frank manner as we have seen no other do better in all our journey'.

The abbot received a very generous pension of £100 a year and the use of 'a mansion house at Coscombe, within the parish of Didbrook with the stable there, a close nearby thereto adjoining and the first vesture of one little meadow adjoining the grove called Coscombe Grove with a little court there' until the King found him a benefice. The house at Coscombe, on the hill above Hailes, had been known as the 'abbot's lodging' and Abbot Sagar had found it a welcome residence while the monastery was functioning. At the time of the Injunctions, which forbade non-residence, he had pleaded with Cromwell, 'I have a disease yearly at fall of leaf and in the summer so that if I may not lie in clear air it will cost me my life'. With the house came forty loads of wood for fires, and timber for house repairs, out of the monastery wood.

Within a few years Sagar had left Gloucestershire for his native north. He became a prebend of York Cathedral and was instituted into a living as a parish priest, eventually being buried beside his brother Otto who had been a corrodian at Hailes at the end. Baddeley said he had seen the abbot's grave at Warmfield in Yorkshire with an inscription: 'We be two brothers, pray you let us rest in peace. Stephen Sagar sometime abbot of Hailes and Otto Sagar vicar of this church'.[7]

Otto's will, which requested this arrangement, was dated 1558, so Stephen must have died before this date.

There is a last glimpse of this diplomatic abbot in a letter written after he had been asked to help settle a dispute between two landowners who had obtained Hailes lands: 'Anthony Dastyn, gentleman, in right of land at Coscombe, and Henry Hodgkins, in right of his farm at Pinnock'. It must have been with a certain wry satisfaction that the abbot heard of quarrels between those who had profited from the rape of Hailes, especially a member of the Dastyn family whose name appeared in no favourable light in the abbey chronicle. Perhaps the words of the Commissioners should serve as Abbot Sagar's epitaph:

We thought it our parts to declare and signify unto your lordships this honest man's behaviour and his doings to the intent that he may at your hand have condign praise and thanks as his full trust in you will do.

The twenty-one monks at Hailes all received pensions which varied from the annual £8 for the Prior, to £2 6s. 6d. for a monk who had been serving as vicar at Longborough. The average pension was £5 a year. Thirteen years after the monastery had come to an end six monks were still receiving their pensions, and two were still alive in 1579. Many monks who had suitable qualifications were given local livings in former churches held by the abbey: Toddington, Pinnock, Longborough, Didbrook; others were at Chedworth, Stanley Pontlarge, Stanton, Fairford and Cirencester. Four monks moved away to Suffolk, the Isle of Wight, Yorkshire and Lichfield. One appears to have married and one returned to monastic life at Westminster (this time as a Benedictine), during the period under Mary Tudor when monastic life was restored there. It is possible that the Cistercian who ended up as a debtor in the Marchelsea prison was one of the same name in the Hailes pensions list.

The matrix of the Seal of the Confraternity of Hailes was found, in 1821, in a perfect state of preservation, in a potato field called Low Garth at Langrick-on-Ouse (Lincoln). It was made of bell metal, oval and 2½ inches long. An abbot's ring was found at Toddington in 1820 but later lost.[8]

The abbey's annual value was estimated at £357 7s 8½d. There were ten recipients of annuities at the abbey including Otto Sagar, the late abbot's brother, and Elizabeth Huddleston, a widow. Objects of gold and silver from the abbey treasury were reserved for the king's use.[9] Of the abbey buildings the church, with aisles, chapel and steeple, the cloister, chapter house, frater, infirmary (with chapel and lodging adjoining), the prior's chamber and the five bells[10] in the church steeple were all 'deemed superfluous' and fated to destruction.

Lead was removed from the roofs of all the buildings assigned for destruction: 119 fodders were sent to Bristol (a fodder was 1950

lbs)[11] to be melted down. Two possible furnace sites for such opera-
tions at Hailes have been uncovered, one in front of the high altar
where a small mound marks the spot.[12] The demolition had reached
its final stage by 1542 when a commission met at Winchcombe to
investigate the unofficial sale of remnants. The records of this
investigation make it possible to piece together the process of
dismantling the fabric. The first lease of the site had gone to Robert
Acton who was responsible to the Crown for demolition. His
servants and their assistants appear to have disposed of much of the
remaining material after the Crown and local gentry had taken their
share.[13] It was at this stage that sections of pavement, including the
Stafford and Melton tiles, were removed to Southam de la Bere,
where the Huddleston family had a house. The list of items disposed
of in small lots reveals the considerable participation of local people
and even former monks. In the words of a monk at Roche Abbey,
Yorkshire, 'I did see all would away and therefore I did as others
did'. People flocked to the site from Didbrook, Winchcombe,
Stanton, Toddington, Stow, Longborough and even Bristol. Loads of
stones were dug from the ground under the paving stones in the
body of the church, cartloads of paper and boards, eleven loads of
paving and ashlar stones, doors, ceiling boards, window frames, iron
bars, piping, washbasins and locks and keys. Some clearly were
worried: there is a record of a maid servant chiding her master for
receiving bags of locks brought to him at night. His reaction echoed
the words of the monk at Roche, 'Catch that may catch'.
Cupboards, a cope chest, a desk, a till, a timber staircase, timber
from the steeple were sold, and sad little items such as a plummet of
lead from a clock, the iron bar that held up the wall going to the
dormitory, and even four little fallen ash trees and three swarms of
bees from the fields around.

A popular item was window glass bought in pieces or by length or
weight. The parson of Stanton was reported to have come with two
great panniers slung over his horse and taken back eighty-six feet of
glass; he also gathered up broken glass pieces. Prices were modest
and the general attitude was that of the master already quoted. It is
understandable that ordinary folk felt entitled to their share of the
spoil when they saw the abbey dismantled before their eyes for the
benefit of the Crown, the local gentry and their agents. Recent
excavations have revealed several thousand surviving tiles and

pavement fragments despite earlier excavations. In places the impression of tiles removed long ago has revealed the site of many sections of the paving of the abbey nave and aisles.

One of the Hailes monks who long survived the end of the abbey was Richard Woodward who became vicar of Chedworth, some sixteen miles south of Hailes and near the Salt Way. (A John Woodward appears among those accused of irregular dealings at Hailes at the sale of the leavings of the abbey.) Richard acquired four little pieces of glass (a keepsake?), and some iron bars. There is nothing startlingly religious about Richard's will; indeed, the usual formal pious introduction is relatively restrained compared with some contemporary wills in the district:

In the name of God AMEN the Xth Day of December in the year of Our Lord 1580, I Richard Woodward, clerk, vicar of Chedworth in the Diocese of Gloucester, being sick in body but whole in mind and perfect of memory do make my last will and testament in manner and form following:

First I bequeath my soul into the hands of Almighty God my Maker and Redeemer and my body to be buried in the church porch of Chedworth.

He left two shillings to the church and one shilling to the poor box. His pension from Hailes had been a hundred shillings, but presumably this ended when he obtained the Chedworth living. His will suggests he maintained a certain Cistercian austerity, by choice or necessity. Except for sixpence each to unspecified godchildren, the total amount of money involved was forty-seven shillings and this included fourpence each, to two overseers and witnesses 'for their pains'. All his books (which suggests he had a number) were bequeathed to a cousin and his long black gown, faced with chamlet, was left to a fellow cleric. Household goods named were more than modest: a mattress, a coverlet, a white coverlet, a cushion, a great pair of tables, a coffer and the table and forms from his hall. More personal were 'my best silver spoon', 'my silver lace', and a pair of skates. Richard's agricultural background is reflected in the sixteen bushels of barley left in varying amounts to villagers, a three-year-old heifer and a malting utensil. His will bears his signature.

Buildings associated with monastic life were to be destroyed completely, but those which could be used for other purposes, largely domestic, were retained. The three inner cloister arches still standing at Hailes, which were part of the rebuilt cloister of the 15th century, were preserved because the former abbot's house and the adjoining kitchens and storerooms were retained as a residence. Local gentry kept an eye on monastic buildings which were to be left undefaced. 'There are three houses in the county of Gloucester of which I should like to have one', wrote a hopeful applicant during the Dissolution. The buildings associated with the abbot's quarters comprised all that was necessary for an elegant country mansion.

Katherine Parr had received the fee of Hailes Abbey as part of her dowry. When she died and was buried at Sudeley Castle it then passed to Thomas Seymour, her second husband and, on his execution, came to his brother-in-law, William Parr. By 1551 John Hodgkins had obtained the lease for twenty-one years, renewing it in 1561. Hodgkins's daughter, Alice, married William Hoby the elder as his second wife. Hoby three times renewed the lease. That of 1594 was granted by Queen Elizabeth 'in consideration of his charge in building and repairing the houses'. The Hoby name appears a number of times in the parish register and there is a tradition that this family repaired and restored the parish church at Hailes which, presumably, had fallen on bad times after the dissolution of the monastery.

William Hoby's death is recorded in the register on 17 March 1602 with the notable entry: 'the days of his age were one hundred and two years'. His will and that of his son of the same name have survived. William the elder's will has a very lengthy introduction:

In the name of God AMEN. I, William Hoby the elder in the County of Gloucester Esq., being in a reasonable state of body and of perfect remembrance, thanks be to Almighty God, being now well stricken in years but putting to remembrance the mortality of every living might do, this thirteenth day of March in the 45th year of Our Sovereign Lady Queen Elizabeth, make and ordain this my last will and testament . . . First, I give and bequeath my soul into the hands of Almighty God trusting through and for the merits of Our Lord Jesus Christ, my Redeemer, to receive at His pardon the absolution of all my sins, and my earthly body to be buried in the chapel of Hayles in such devout and comely manner as to my executor or sureties shall seem expedient, hoping at the general Day of Judgement to rise both in body and soul and be among those eternal and celestial joys which Almighty God hath in His mercy provided for His elect and chosen.'

Alice, his wife and executor, was well provided for. Particularly interesting are the individual items of plate mentioned among William's bequests to his family. They include:

My best basin and cover of silver gilt
Two broad gilt bowls
A round basin with a silver cover
Two dozen gilt spoons
Two pair salts, gilt
Two silver jugs parcel gilt
Four silver candle sticks
My two silver jugs, parcel gilt, worked with the letters W.H.

A standing cup of gilt, with its cover, was left to his daughter-in-law, Mary, for her life and to her then unborn child. The value of his plate is indicated by William's request that his eldest son Giles (who was to have property elsewhere), should receive the sum of £200 instead of plate promised to him. The abbot's hall must have been resplendent when William's gold and silver plate was on display after the custom of the time.

More mundane household items give some impression of the interior of the Hoby house: bedsteads, tables, joined stools, items of brass and ironwork all considered worthy of mention, together with furniture of the brewhouse, cellars and buttery. References to a mill, malting house, carts and wains, and instruments of husbandry at Hailes and nearby Pinnock, with confirmation of agreements already made of the grazing of a large flock of sheep on the Cotswolds, complete the rural scene little changed since the monks were there. William, already a man when the monastery was dissolved, clearly wanted its existence remembered for he made a proviso that the glass, wainscot, locks, keys and door should remain undefaced.

Sir John Tracy was one of the overseers of the wills of both William Hobys. Mary Tracy was married to William the younger who survived his father by a single day. Alice, his mother, died in 1607 and the Tracy family then acquired Hailes and lived in the abbot's house for most of the 17th century before returning to their Toddington home. The family fought on the Royalist side in the Civil War. In 1642 Charles I granted Sir John Tracy the barony and viscountcy of Tracy of Rathcoole, County Dublin. The Hailes parish register shows the impact of the war with a note inserted in 1656 stating: 'This register was neglected about ten years until Mr Henry Winde was instituted'. He had been deprived by parliamentary ordinance from a Worcestershire living but lived to serve at Hailes until his death in 1706. The Tracy family also felt the consequences of the Civil War, beign forced to pay two thousand pounds between 1648 and 1665 to redeem their sequestered property.

In 1685 the Rev. John Matthews came as domestic chaplain to the third Viscount and perhaps also served the parish church. He recorded in his diary his arrival at Hailes just before Christmas and wrote warmly of the 'regular government of the family, the constant good table and the kindly treatment of the servants who were well fed and went to bed betimes.' Lord Tracy was generous in lending his books and papers so that his chaplain was able to study in peace and prepare discourses which were well received. Matthews preached once on Sundays and read the service daily. There were few visitors to the house during the Christmas period but those who came were very well entertained.

John was not long able to enjoy being 'generously and respectfully used by the heads of the family', for Lord Tracy, then approaching his seventy-first year, died suddenly. His chaplain wrote that he had had forebodings for some weeks and observed that the old man only dined once a day but then ate to repletion. The parish register records. 'The Right Hon'able John, Lord Viscount Tracy dyed at Hailes and was buried at Toddington' 11 March 1687. His will was dated 3 March, 1682.

Among the domestic fragments excavated at Hailes over the years has been a number of those precious keys which William Hoby had been so anxious to preserve. There were fragments of late 16th- and even more 17th-century pottery and china. These, with personal items such as buttons (one showing a horses head in relief) a child's thimble, and part of a belt-fitting, bring us near the busy households of the Hobys and Tracys. A number of clay pipes found especially in the kitchen area, and most of late 17th-century date, is a reminder that tobacco was grown here, still recalled in a piece of land called 'Tobacco Piece'.[14]

A few years after John Matthews had left, Hailes was visited by the famous traveller and diarist, Celia Fiennes.

She does not record if the Tracy family had remained in residence after the death of the third viscount, only referring to the 'better house with a park' which the family had at Toddington. Of the Hailes house she observes 'it is a good old house and there is a pretty chapel with a gallery for people of quality to sit in which goes out of the hall that is a lofty large room'. It has been suggested that when the lay brothers disappeared in the 14th century their disused *necessarium* may have been converted or rebuilt into a chapel. Kip's view of *c.* 1712 would appear to support this.

Lyson's view of the ruins in 1794, showing the remains of the west range with part of the cloister beyond.

It is difficult to know the fate of the house when the Tracy family returned to their old home at Toddington. Four views of the abbey survive to witness its decay. Kip's view shows the mansion complete with evidence of the battlemented tower at the south-west end. Foundations of this tower, unbounded and tacked on at an uncertain date, were recently uncovered. Buck's engraving of 1732 shows, from the position of the former chapter house, the way in which the abbot's house extended over the cloister walk and the kitchen area to the site of the *frater*. The building is revealed as many-gabled. Anne Tracy rode over from Stanway in 1723 and rambled all over the empty building. The most evocative view of Hailes in the mid-18th century is that of Thomas Robins, the elder, whose water colour (see cover) shows the house and its setting, with part of the old barn and the parish church visible. When Lysons drew his romantic sketch in 1794 the house appears to have perished except for part of the tower and some cloister arches. He recorded in 1804 that 'some of the offices and the barn are standing'.

When the Tracy family moved to Toddington early in the 18th century, or a little before, they took with them from Hailes some of the stained glass windows which had decorated the former abbot's house; these are recorded as having included roundels with the eagle

Victorian visitors from a London archaeological society seen near the west cloister walk.
Illustrated Times, 16 August 1856.

of Richard as King of the Romans, with an inscription referring to him as 'august founder' of the abbey, his arms as Earl of Cornwall and the royal arms.[15] The arms of Huddleston were also found. In the windows of a former church at Toddington there was some good 15th-century glass from the abbey, illustrating the Apostles' Creed. When a new church was built towards the end of the 19th century this glass was removed and put away in a box in the estate office. It was returned to Hailes in 1903 and is now in the east window of the parish church.[16] A family pew with original iron hinges and linen-fold panels almost certainly came from the abbey (a cupboard with similar panelling was until recently at Toddington and other similar panels were known at Didbrook and Winchcombe). Few houses around Hailes were without stone and other remnants from the abbey built into walls or used to decorate gardens. Some of the stone was used as foundation for roads in the district.

The abbey museum and annexe provide evidence enough for the glory that was Hailes in architecture, tiles and sculpture. Because of its rural site more has survived than might be expected, unlike Winchcombe where the site was so flattened and ploughed up as early as the 17th century that even a knowledgeable antiquarian of the time was not able to discern the exact layout.

In the modern Cistercian abbey at Mount St Bernard, Leicestershire, is a statue referred to as 'the Black Madonna of Hailes'. Bought in 1840, with some furniture from a farmhouse thought to have been connected with Hailes, it came into the hands of a nephew of the original purchaser who sent it to Clifton whence it reached Mount St Bernard.

Fragmentary evidence for the survival of some of the buildings helps shed a little more light. The Inquisition post-mortem on Sir William Hoby records the existence at Hailes of 'one inn with appurtenances, certain houses and buildings, a dovecote and a pool'. The inn was still standing in Victorian times when it was described as a courtyard building entered by an arch. This was presumably the old pilgrim hostelry. There is also reference to a large old building near the abbey house. In 1615 the parish register records the death at Hailes of 'a poor travelling man born at the grange'. In 1660 a child was drowned in the fish pond. In 1707 a 'poor man born in Hailes barn', formerly a receptacle for beggars, 'after seventy years of vagrancy was sent back to Hailes with a pass'. The old barn survived into this century and was used as the abbey museum until the present one was built. 'A very memorable old pigeon-house' at Hailes was recalled by a member of the Tracy family in the 19th century.

Britton in 1840 recorded that the site of the cloister and house were then part of a farm. The crinolined and parasol-burdened figures of Victorian visitors with their top-hatted escorts, shown in the *Illustrated Times* of August 1856 recording the visit of an antiquarian society from London, indicated the site well grown with trees and undergrowth. By the late 19th century *The Strangers' Guide to Cheltenham* was warning visitors who 'have a desire to contemplate these ruins':

let them take good heed that they follow not the ensnaring directions about the whereabouts of Hailes Abbey or the distance thereof or else they may fall into the error of others who after seeking the assurance from a decent countryman that the place they sought was to be found by turning at a certain point found themselves after two hours hard walking rather more than a mile on a road opposite the one on which they should have been.

These Victorian adventurers must have felt like the founding monks when they arrived but, whereas the former had thought 'how awful is this place', the Victorians fell in love with its romantic charm: 'The ruins of the abbey like the charms of a village beauty are covered with a wimple of nature's making'.

In 1876 the British Archaeological Association inspected the ruins and the speaker expressed the wish that the owner of the property would cause the ruins to be excavated and the foundations laid bare. From 1899 to 1908, Canon William Bazeley and W. St Clair Baddeley undertook the work of excavation with generous contributions from the Bristol and Gloucestershire Archaeological Society. The Economic Life Assurance Society spent fifty pounds renovating the ancient barn as a museum, which the B.G.A.S. furnished, while trustees were appointed to protect the site and museum. The wages of the labourers for the sessions 1899 to 1900 totalled £135 1s. 8d., a tent cost £3, and the custodian's salary was £8 5s! Baddeley's privately printed *A Cotteswold Shrine* (350 copies, 1908) was a splendid record of one man's love affair with Hailes.

In the late 1920s, Sir James Fowler, formerly custodian of the mother house at Beaulieu, became custodian of Hailes. He did much to clear the site of undergrowth and ivy, marking out the plan of the abbey again. He was responsible for building the present museum and starting the collection of the scattered relics of the abbey. To encourage visitors he persuaded the Great Western Railway to provide a halt on the Cheltenham-Honeybourne line. The railway cottages stand near the bridge on the lane from the main Cheltenham-Broadway road. Sir James planted the trees which until recently marked the site of the pillars of the nave of the abbey church.

The National Trust were given the site by the Andrews family of Toddington and, in 1948, the Ministry of Works (later the Department of the Environment, and now English Heritage) were constituted Guardians of the abbey.

Seven hundred years have passed since the pioneer monks from Beaulieu Abbey completed their momentous journey to Hailes to establish the monastery which its Founder, Richard, Earl of Cornwall, determined to build in great splendour and where he and most of his family still lie. The serenity of the place still reflects the words of a great Cistercian saint inscribed in Latin on the north cloister walls:

It is good for us to be here where man lives more purely, falls more rarely, rises more speedily, proceeds more surely, dies more happily, is sooner purified and more richly rewarded. *St Bernard*

REFERENCES

Chapter 1. The Founder of Hailes Abbey

1. Matthew (1200-59) monk of the Benedictine abbey of St Albans, a lively and candid commentator and historian of the contemporary scene, knew most of the outstanding men of the age and delighted to relate details of events they had described to him, often adding evocative marginal drawings. Henry III is recorded as having on one state occasion asked Matthew to be sure to note every detail for posterity. Matthew knew Richard and conversed with him. He was probably present at the dedication of Hailes abbey. His Great Chronicle has a lively sketch of the French prisoners freeing themselves from their shackles while their prison door is flung triumphantly open.

2. It has been suggested that the lion rampant in the centre of the arms of Richard may derive from Poitou.

3. Matthew Paris explains it thus: 'The kingdom of Germany is called the Roman kingdom because it was, as it were, a pledge given for obtaining the Holy Roman Empire.'

4. One of Richard's sisters married the King of Scotland and another Frederick II. Richard visited the latter in Sicily on his return from his Crusade and seems to have told Matthew Paris all about it, enabling the monk to provide two delightful drawings of the elephants sent to greet him and two Saracen girls who danced to music on revolving balls as part of his entertainment.

5. A long-cross silver penny of Henry III was found in excavations in 1972-3 in the footings of the frater at Hailes. Steelyard weights of the time bear Richard's arms: one survives at Sudeley Castle.

6. The Household Accounts of the Countess show that she took trouble for the comfort of her imprisoned brothers, sending for dates, raisins, spices, sugar and whalemeat (for Lent?). Scarlet cloth with miniver hood for Richard and striped cloth with satin hood for Edmund were purchased for their wardrobes.

7. Young Henry was not imprisoned and the Hailes chronicler relates how he succeeded in capturing in a skirmish the Earl of Derby who was a friend of the Montfort cousins, seeing this as a possible reason for the murder.

8. Notebook in Baddeley Collection.

9. A silver gilt sceptre topped by a dove, attributed to Richard, was on display at the Age of Chivalry Exhibition, 1987-8 (*Catalogue*, no 14, p. 203). A seal showing him enthroned with orb and sceptre and inscribed *Ricardus dei gratia Romanorum rex semper Augustus* survives on a Cologne charter. The same inscription appeared on a stained glass window from the abbey. This was later placed in the hall at Old Toddington. It appears to have been sold abroad in 1893.

10. Popular ballads of the day were merciless in their verses about the part he played in the battle and accused him of trickery in all his dealings. A mob attacked his home near London.

11. The portrait of Beatrix (d. 1277) with her coat of arms in stained glass, was placed in the church of the Friars Minor at Oxford. It is thought to be the earliest surviving donor figure in English glass. It is now in the Burrell Collection, Pollok Park, Glasgow. Beatrix's arms are painted on the south chancel wall of the parish church at Hailes and appear on tiles from the abbey.

Chapter 2. The Foundation and Building of the Monastery

1.   Henry III spent more than £40,000 on Westminster between 1245 and his death in 1272. £18,000 was spent on work there between 1246 and 1255, the period when building was in progress at Hailes.

2.   Matthew Paris mistakenly gives thirteen monks but the Waverley chronicler agrees with the Hailes figures.

3.   Winchcombe, Gloucester, Deerhurst, Tewkesbury, Pershore, Evesham, Malvern and Worcester were all Benedictine. There were Augustinian canons in Gloucester and Cirencester while Templars and Hospitallers were to be found at Guiting and Quenington. The nearest Cistercian houses were at Kingswood, Tintern and Flaxley.

4.   Or Shilton?

5.   Variously spelt as Heile, Helis, Heyles, Hayles, Hailles, Haylus, Hales, the origin of the name has been much debated, being variously seen as derived from *sal* (dirty) or *salenses* (folk living near a stream).

6.   Elsewhere in the chronicle called Grove Mill.

7.   Didbrook does not appear in Domesday.

8.   The bosses retain some of their original colour. The bosses and vaulting at Pershore Abbey give a good idea of how these bosses would have looked *in situ*.

9.   It has been suggested that John of Waverley, who had worked for Henry III and was a lay-brother, may have been the Hailes *cementarius* (mason). John of Gloucester is another possible candidate.

10.   One of the miracles recorded by the sixteenth-century monk of Hailes refers to pits left by limeburners, and quarries pitting the ground adjoining Pyseley Hill, near the Salt Way above Hailes. See Chapter 3.

11.   The cloister museum illustrates many of these details.

12.   A mark was 13s. 4d., approximately 67p.

13.   The records of Flaxley Abbey indicate that the King eventually had to curb his generosity in the matter of oaks for monastic building for he substituted the gift of a wood 'because the Oaks were becoming depleted'. A rosary bead which had fallen under Henry's oak choir stalls was found on the site of the monastic choir.

14.   The cooking of meat in the monks' kitchen was forbidden by the Rule so a place was set apart where sick and elderly monks could have a meat diet (*misericordia*, compassion).

15.   Richard's love of pageantry is evident. His introduction of Sanchia to London was a splendid occasion. The city was decorated with hangings, curtains and divers other ornaments, while his marriage feast was followed by so much nuptial conviviality that even Matthew Paris was unable to do justice to the entertainment. 'There were thirty thousand dishes to be got ready for those who sat down to dinner,' he marvelled.

16.   The Tudor historian and traveller, Leland, recorded seeing her memorial in the presbytery at Cirencester. The money she bequeathed to that abbey was used by Abbot Adam for the use of pittances there — a pleasant way to ensure that she was remembered. (A pittance was an extra allowance of food or similar 'treat'.)

17.   There was no diocese of Gloucester until after the Reformation.

18.   Included among the archives of Edmund is an account (1292-3) recording 100 marks (£66 13s. 4d.) given to Thomas, Treasurer of Hailes Abbey, and Master Berenger, *cementarius* for the works of that church. A further donation was recorded for the same purpose (see *Catalogue* of Age of Chivalry Exhibition, no. 443, p. 392).

19.   The practice of divided burial originated in the desire to secure the maximum opportunity for prayers to be said for the dead. It was forbidden by a papal bull of Boniface VIII (1294-1303).

20.   'In his treasury what seemed like an almost infinite amount of gold and silver and precious stones was found.' *Bury Chronicle*.

Chapter 3. The Holy Blood

1. The significance of the relic can be judged by a sermon given by the contemporary Bishop of Norwich in which he declared 'of all things held sacred the most precious is the Blood of Christ, for it was the price of the world and the shedding of it was the salvation of the world'.

2. Henry III carried a similar relic from old St Paul's to Westminster, 'attended by robed priests and clerks carrying crosses and lighted tapers walking under a canopy raised on four spears. In his hand wrapped in a cloth he held aloft the relic, his arms supported, his eyes uplifted despite the unevenness of the way.' Matthew Paris.

3. William of Gloucester was much involved in Henry III's work on the shrine at Westminster which, Matthew says, was made of the purest gold and costly pearls but, even then 'the workmanship outshone the fabric'.

4. The so-called Buckland Cope has embroidered on its border a church with transepts, a central tower and spire, and what appears to be a monstrance, probably representing the Holy Blood. (Buckland church, near Broadway, Worcs.)

5. Henry III granted £20 a year for keeping four wax candles about the shrine at Westminster, in addition to the lights already there, and made provision for 300 for Christmas and other feasts. It is likely that Edmund, who gave the relic and almost certainly was responsible for the building of the chevet, made similar provision for Hailes.

6 and 7. Tiles bearing the arms of both families have been found.

8. It is probably this story which is referred to in 'The Fantasy of Idolatory':

> To the Holy Blood of Hayles
> With your fingers and your nayles
> And That ye may stretch and Wynne
> Yet it would not be seen
> Except you were shriven
> And clear of all deadly synne

9. Walsingham brought in £250 and Canterbury £36 annually.

Chapter 4. The Early Years of the Monastery

1. The records of Tewkesbury abbey give a vivid impression of the disturbance which multitudes of mourners and sightseers could cause by attending the elaborate funerals of noble laymen and women. At least one of their patrons was buried secretly at night for fear of the noisy intrusion of the crowds.

2. His tomb survives at Worcester.

3. The north door of the parish church was probably blocked when the villagers were moved.

4. 'They wear nothing with furs or linen, neither breeches unless on a journey when they wash and return them to store on their return.' Cistercians slept girded and fully clad, rose early, laboured hard, never missed services and maintained the rule of silence. No meat or lard was eaten at meals and from September to Easter they took only one meal a day. The abbot lived austerely with his monks, slept in the common dormitory and dined with guests in the refectory. In the twelfth century William of Malmesbury had observed them with admiration: 'They prefer shining minds to vestments' he wrote.

5. Richard of Cornwall had provided for alms to be given to the poor, and bread and herrings on Sunday.

6.　The monastery walls at Beaulieu were constructed of rubble and reached ten feet in height and $2^3/4$ feet in width. The gateways have survived there as they have at Kingswood in Gloucestershire. Hailes presumably had Cotswold walling and perhaps earthen banks to mark its boundaries.

7.　Many accounts of the abbey history refer to a great fire at Hailes in 1271, which certainly would have contributed to the decision to extend the church. The abbey chronicles make no mention of such an event whereas they carefully record fires at Evesham and Llanthony. So far there is no archaeological evidence to support this story.

8.　John Carter is recorded as keeping four hundred sheep on former monastery ground at Swell in the 17th century.

9.　The settlement was in the form of a chirograph, a written indenture copied several times on a single sheet then divided so that each of the parties concerned had a copy.

10.　The charter mentions that the Earl had a little fishpond there 'which should not cause the condition of the mill to deteriorate'.

11.　Such tally sticks were usually made of hazel wood and notches of varying width and depth recorded on its edges the sums involved. The stick would then be cut lengthwise, giving each party a record of the transaction. In 1272 the abbot had the right of Court Leet and goods of felons at Pinnock, and this was allowed in 1287. The £6 6s. 10d. annual rent had been settled on Margaret of Anjou by Edward I in 1298-9, on his marriage. Early in the 15th century a monk of Hailes was installed at Pinnock church because the living was too poor to attract a priest. The church was not appropriated to the abbey but it had the right of presentation. At the Dissolution, a Hailes monk, the abbey kitchener, was priest there. An interesting entry in the parish church register of Hailes reveals that the church of Pinnock was 'demolished time immemorial'. A baptism took place at a farmhouse at Pinnock.

12.　Beaulieu's share was £13.

13.　Edward's presence at Hailes at this time may be the reason for the appearance of the arms of his first wife, Eleanor of Castille, in the parish church. The *fleur de lys* and marguerites in stained glass which survive there may be a compliment to his second wife, Margaret of France.

Chapter 5. Hailes Parish Church

1.　Winchcombe abbey had a field chapel at Hailes by the 12th century. A certain Ralph of Worcester built a castle at Hailes and a church which is probably the present one. There was a bitter dispute with Winchcombe (about parochial rights) which only ended after long litigation and eventual compromise. The foundation charter of Hailes gave it the advowson of the church which came with the manor. Soon afterwards the abbey took possession (advowson, right of patronage).

2.　The arms read chronologically from bottom to top.

3.　Richard's sister married the King of Scotland.

4.　The Honour of St Valery (in the Thames valley) belonged to Richard.

5.　Richard's first wife, the widow of Gilbert de Clare, Earl of Gloucester, died in childbirth before the abbey was founded. Edmund, Sanchia's son, married Margaret de Clare although that marriage was annulled. Many de Clare tiles belong to the abbey.

6.　The windows were clearly inserted into older walls during massive rebuilding after the abbey took over the Norman church.

7.　Originally these scenes, set in an architectural framework of alternating round and pointed arches with dividing pinnacles, were painted over the intervening wooden struts, making a continuous frieze which probably extended into the nave.

8.   There are animal grotesques on some of the tiles found in the abbey church. Edmund had at least one scribe who kept accounts of his Wallingford estates and enlivened his labours with marginal drawings of strange creatures.

St Bernard, the great Cistercian saint, would not have approved. He protested vigorously about the use of such grotesques in churches and monasteries: 'These creatures half beast half man . . . here a quadruped with a serpent's head, there an animal half man half goat . . . if we do not blush at such absurdities we should at least regret what we spend upon them.'

9.   The huntsman's shield has been twice delineated, with three horns and three sea horses.

Chapter 6. The Middle Years

1.   The Abbot of Beaulieu, in a visitation of Hailes, had forbidden the keeping of hunting dogs by the monks in the abbey, although they were allowed on the granges.
2.   The Bishop of Worcester in 1321 had written to the King to seek to excuse himself for absence from a council meeting in London 'on account of floods which in our parts have been worse than elsewhere and on account of the danger of the roads not clear of evil-doers'.
3.   'To bring to their own use'. The monastery received the greater tithes (wheat sheaves, crops, beasts) as rector, but had to provide a vicar to see to the spiritual needs of the parishioners. The vicar was entitled to the lesser tithes (natural produce and the results of men's work: apples, acorns, honey, felled trees, issue of animals and products of men's skills). The Lateran Council of 1215 drew attention to the evils of the system: underpaid vicars and neglected parishes. There were 136 appropriated churches in the Worcester diocese in 1291.
4.   A corrody was technically board and lodging granted to a layman in return for a lump sum. The Crown found the system a useful way of helping superannuated royal servants.
5.   The White Book of Worcester records the sturdy resistance of the abbey to these demands.
6.   Beaulieu paid £23 6s. 8d. and Kingswood £13 6s. 8d.
7.   In the last century horses bred at Hailes were a special feature at the horse fairs at Winchcombe, held in March and July.
8.   Beaulieu and Tintern paid 54s. 4d. while Kingswood paid only 26s. 8d. and Flaxley 20s.
9.   Medieval abbots were often called away on business or to sit in Parliament. The abbot of Hailes was a mitred abbot. See the Melton tiles in the abbey museum which show crozier and mitre.
10. As Cistercians they were exempt from visitation by the bishop or his deputy. When a Cistercian abbot took office he swore subjection, reverence and obedience to the bishop according to the Rule of St Benedict, but added the proviso 'saving our perpetual Order'. The bishop could visit (or claim expenses for a visit to) churches under the care of the monastery. There is evidence that this was done in the case of Hailes' churches.
11. *Archives Departmentales*, Côte d'Or.

Chapter 7. Recovery

1.   One is built into the wall of Greet Manor, near Winchcombe.
2.   The first route was that taken by the baker of Stow and his family in the miracle told by the monk of Hailes in the 16th century. The second was the route of the processions of the Holy Blood in 1270 and the funeral of Edmund in 1301.

3. The Buckland Cope which is made from two vestments includes embroidered details of all three.
4. Said to have been the blood of Lancastrians fleeing from the Battle of Tewkesbury. Damage to the doors said to have been done at the same time is more likely to have been the work of the local militia in the last century.
5. See the engravings by Kip and Buck.

Chapter 8. The Last Days of Hailes

1. Also called Whalley from his place of origin. The abbot of Whalley, before he was hanged for sympathy with the Northern Rising of 1537, is reported to have sent a message to Sagar saying he would 'be glad to see him once more ere I depart this world, seeing I brought him up as a boy'.
2. Duns Scotus was a 14th-century scholastic, a contemporary of Thomas Aquinas with whom he had been involved in vigorous debate.
3. The former abbot of Waverley, whose abbey was dissolved in 1536, left books to two Hailes monks he had met at Oxford when he became Provisor of St Bernard College.
4. Boiling.
5. The letter was signed by Bishop Latimer; Henry, Prior of Worcester; Stephen, Abbot of Hailes; and Richard Tracy, their four seals being attached.
6. Possibly that mentioned in Lady Huddleston's will.
7. *A Cotteswold Shrine.*
8. Between the church and the house.
9. These included mitres garnished with silver gilt, small pearls and counterfeit stones, gold and silver plate and one copy of blue tissue with one chasuble and one tunicle of the same material.
10. The abbey's bells, weighing 944 lbs, 1065 lbs, 1281 lbs, 1511 lbs and 2016 lbs, are last recorded as 'standing on the green at Hailes'. The largest bell was broken and would have needed recasting. Leave was given for the bells to be sent to Stratford-upon-Avon but there is no evidence that they arrived.
11. At St Osyth's, Essex, in 1539, a fodder was valued at £4. The plumber responsible for melting it down received 5s.
12. Baddeley recorded: 'We found a cupellation furnace, burnt stones, and splashes of lead everywhere, the basin being deeply reddened. It was set fast into the clay of the grave of Henry of Alemagne.'
13. 'When the abbey was dissolved the ornaments such as painted glass and bricks (tiles) were collected by the neighbouring gentry and applied as embellishments of their houses.' Bigland.
14. The Tracys of Toddington and Hailes were involved with others in a scheme launched in 1619 for tobacco-growing in the area.
15. Richard's arms, as Earl of Cornwall, also survive in a top light in the east window of Hailes church and in modern glass at Toddington.
16. At the base of this window are two inscriptions which record the travels of the glass. The delicately etched one on the left side came from the former church at Toddington and records the re-leading of the window with the figures from Hailes Abbey by Viscount Tracy in 1789. That on the right hand side records the return of the glass to Hailes by Mr Hugh Andrews, the later owner of Toddington. The figures of the apostles, with their scrolls each bearing a section of the Creed, are not now complete.

SELECT BIBLIOGRAPHY

Sources

Chronicle of Hailes Abbey, MS.BL Cleopatra D3

Chronicle of Hailes Abbey, MS.BL Harley 3725

Matthew Paris: *Chronica Majora*, ed. H. R. Luard. 7 vols. Rolls Series, 1872-83

Annales Monastici (AD 1-1432), ed. H. R. Luard. 5 vols. Rolls Series, 1864-9

William Dugdale: *Monasticon Anglicanum*. Vol. 5. Reprinted in 6 vols, 1846

Episcopal Registers of Worcester Diocese: Bishop Gifford, ed. Bund (1902); Bishop Cobham, ed. Pearce (1930); Bishop Reynolds, ed. Wilson (1927); Bishop Gainsborough, ed. Bund (1905); Sede Vacante, ed. Bund (1893)

The Baddeley Collection (Gloucester City Library)

Valor Ecclesiasticus. Henry VIII auctoritate regia institutus. 6 vols. Record Commission, 1810-34

Sir Robert Atkyns, *Ancient and Present State of Glostershire* (1712)

R. Bigland, *Historical Monuments and Genealogical Collections relative to the County of Gloucester* (1791)

D. Royce, ed. *Landboc sive Registrum Monasterii Beatae Mariae Virginis et Sancti Cenhelmi de Winchelcumba.* 2 vols (Exeter 1892-1903)

S. Rudder, *A New History of Gloucestershire* (Cirencester 1779)

S. H. Smith: *Place Names of Gloucestershire* (1964-5)

Victoria County History, Gloucestershire: Vol. 2 (1907)

Yorkshire Archaeological Journal, Vols 9-10, 15

Gloucestershire Notes and Queries

Transactions of the Bristol and Gloucestershire Archaeological Society

Further Reading

G. Baskerville, *English Monks and the Suppression of the Monasteries* (1937)

H. S. Braun, *English Abbeys* (1971)

C. Brooke, *The Monastic World* (1974)

G. H. Cook, *English Monasteries in the Middle Ages* (1961)

G. H. Cook, *Letters to Cromwell and others on the Suppression of the Monasteries* (1965)

O. Cook and E. Smith, *English Abbeys and Priories* (1960)

G. G. Coulton, *Five Centuries of Religion Vols 1-4* (1923-50)

J. C. Dickinson, *Monastic Life in Medieval England* (1961)

E. S. Eames, *Medieval Tiles* (1985)

Sir James Fowler, *Hayles and Beaulieu: a brief history and guide to Hayles Abbey* (1928)

R. A. R. Hartridge, *A History of Vicarages in the Middle Ages* (1930)

Dom Frederick Hockey, *Beaulieu, King John's Abbey: a history of Beaulieu Abbey, Hampshire 1204-1538* (1976)

Dom David Knowles, *The Religious Orders in England.* 3 vols (1948-59)

Dom David Knowles, *Bare Ruined Choirs* (1977)

W. R. Lethaby, *Westminster Abbey and the King's Craftsmen: a study in medieval building* (1906)

C. Platt, *The Monastic Grange in Medieval England: a reassessment* (1969)

C. Platt, *The Abbeys and Priories of Medieval England* (1984)

Sir F. M. Powicke, *Oxford History of England: The Thirteenth Century 1216-1307* (1953)